TEST ITEM FILE
GORDON MORK

NINTH EDITION

A HISTORY OF CIVILIZATION

ROBIN W. WINKS

CRANE BRINTON
JOHN B. CHRISTOPHER
ROBERT LEE WOLFF

Prentice Hall, *Upper Saddle River, New Jersey 07458*

© 1996 by PRENTICE-HALL, INC.
Simon & Schuster / A Viacom Company
Upper Saddle River, New Jersey 07458

All rights reserved

10 9 8 7 6 5 4 3 2 1

ISBN 0-13-228354-9
Printed in the United States of America

A NOTE TO THE INSTRUCTOR

Though testing is not the be-all and end-all of education, instructors have an obligation, I believe, to provide some means to determine their students' level of achievement. This TEST ITEM FILE will provide you with materials to do just that.

You will find a combination of multiple choice, true/false, and essay items. It is my belief that each form has its place in a balanced history course. In the best of all possible worlds, one might argue that all testing would be oral conversation or essay writing, and that all such individual tests would always be objectively and consistently graded. But we know that such a circumstance is impossible. The Educational Testing Service's Advanced Placement program, for example, combines multiple choice and essay (or "free response") questions in its European History program, the closest thing to a "national" test we have in the United States on the topic being addressed here.

Each multiple choice and true/false item has with it the correct answer based on this textbook, and the page number for reference to the NINTH EDITION of the book. The essay exams, on the other hand, have no such references, because there is not a single "model" for a correct answer, and the material for an appropriate answer is not contained in any single page, or group of pages. You will find some guidance for high quality essay answers by referring to the comments in the INSTRUCTOR'S MANUAL as well as in the textbook itself. Some instructors find that if they give students a list of thoughtful questions to practice upon early in the semester, they will get improved answers at testing time. The items listed at the end of each chapter under the heading CRITICAL THINKING (a new feature in this edition) will be very useful for this purpose.

This new edition of the TEST ITEM FILE has been coordinated with the NINTH EDITION of the Winks, Brinton, Christopher, and Wolff textbook and with Mork's accompanying INSTRUCTOR'S MANUAL. I wish to acknowledge the work of Miles W. Cambell and Lynda L. Phillips on earlier editions of the TEST ITEM FILE, and the help of Chris Truelsen, my undergraduate intern. The overall guidelines for this project have been set by the editors of Prentice Hall.

While using this material, you may wish to let me know what you think of it and to make suggestions for improvement. I would be pleased to hear from you.

Gordon R. Mork
Purdue University

CHAPTER 1: THE FIRST CIVILIZATIONS

1.-.1: Anthropologists have found significant fossil evidence of early humanlike animal forms from more than 14 million years ago in

(a) Germany's Neander Valley.
(b) a cave near Peking, China.
(c) Java.
(d) east-central Africa.

(d) p. 5

1.-.2: Known to use stone tools and ritual burial practices, this culture was based on hunting and gathering food.

(a) Neanderthal
(b) Paleolithic
(c) New Stone Age
(d) Peking man

(a) p. 5

1.-.3: The major event which divides prehistory from history was the introduction of

(a) agriculture.
(b) domesticated animals.
(c) written records.
(d) village life.

(c) p. 5

1.-.4: Which of the following cultural traits was NOT found in the Old Stone Age?

(a) human burials
(b) bronze production
(c) calendars
(d) cave paintings

(b) p. 6

1.-.5 Humanity's transition from the Paleolithic (Old Stone Age) period to the Neolithic (New Stone Age) was marked by

(a) the construction of permanent dwellings.
(b) the cultivation of plants for food.
(c) the domestication of animals for food.
(d) all of the above.

(d) p. 7

1.-.6: New Stone Age culture appeared first in

(a) central Africa.
(b) the Near East.
(c) central Asia.
(d) the Danube basin.

(b) p. 7

1.-.7: The first appearance of the New Stone Age occurred about

(a) 1,000,000 years ago.
(b) 25,000 years ago.
(c) 8000 B.C.
(d) 3200 B.C.

(c) p. 7

1.-.8: Archaeological evidence indicates that the art of writing was first seen in

(a) Iran.
(b) Anatolia.
(c) Egypt.
(d) Mesopotamia.

(d) p. 9

1.-.9: Recognizing changing place names in history are important because

(a) accuracy is essential in geography.
(b) changes are confusing and should be avoided whenever possible.
(c) each place has only one real name.
(d) political events often lead to changes in names.

(a) p. 8

1.-.10: The earliest system of writing was probably developed by the
(a) Egyptians.
(b) neolithic people of Jericho.
(c) Subarians.
(d) Akkadians.

(c) p. 9

1.-.11: Earliest governments among the Sumerians was in the hands of

(a) "god-kings."
(b) warrior monarchs.
(c) councils of elders.
(d) priests.

(c) p. 10

1.-.12: Ur-Nammu was the

(a) unifier of Egypt.
(b) first known lawgiver.
(c) earliest "empire-builder."
(d) hero of the Gilgamesh epic.

(b) p. 10

1.-.13: Which of the following was NOT a threat to the Sumerians?

(a) the Semites of Arabia
(b) the rulers of Akkad
(c) the Egyptians
(d) the Elamites

(c) p. 11

1.-.14: In Sumerian society, the ziggurat was the center of

(a) administration
(b) foreign trade
(c) religious activity
(d) agriculture

(c) p. 12

1.-.15: "When the seventh day dawned the storm from the south subsided, the sea grew calm, the flood was stilled. I looked at the face of the world and there was silence, all mankind was turned to clay." This early account similar to that of Noah's ark and the great flood, is found in the

(a) Book of the Dead.
(b) Code of Hammurabi.
(c) Iliad.
(d) Gilgamesh Epic.

(d) p. 11

1.-.16: The Code of Hammurabi revealed a

(a) basically democratic society.
(b) stern system of justice.
(c) communistic economy.
(d) society without slavery.

(b) p. 12

1.-.17: Which of the following was NOT an achievement of Babylonian-Assyrian culture?

(a) advanced mathematics
(b) astronomical observations
(c) rejection of magic
(d) codification of laws

(c) p. 13

1.-.18: A harsh, militaristic people, their empire extended from the Black and Mediterranean Seas to Babylonia.

(a) Philistines
(b) Assyrians
(c) Hittites
(d) Phoenicians

(b) p. 14

1.-.19: The kingdom over which Kings Nebuchadnezzar and Belshazzar had ruled fell in 539 B.C. to

(a) the Egyptians.
(b) Cyrus the Great of Persia.
(c) the Hurrians.
(d) Tiglath-pileser III.

(b) p. 13

1.-.20: Egyptian and Mesopotamian societies had in common the fact that both

(a) were hydraulic societies.
(b) lacked organized priesthoods.
(c) were easily unified.
(d) were ethnically Indo-Aryans.

(a) p. 13

1.-.21: The unifier of Egypt was said to have been

(a) Ramses III.
(b) Akhenaten.
(c) Menes.
(d) Horus.

(c) p. 13

1.-.22: A major factor in the fall of the Old Kingdom of Egypt was

(a) the Hyksos invasion.
(b) prolonged droughts due to decreasing rainfall.
(c) the "revolution" begun by Akhenaten.
(d) the growing independence of local governors.

(d) p. 13

1.-.23: The Hyksos invaders of Egypt were

(a) Asian chariot-warriors.

(b) nomads from the Sahara.
(c) one of the "Sea-peoples."
(d) from the Sudan region.

(a) p. 14

1.-.24: The pharaoh Amenhotep IV (Akhenaten) created a "revolution" in Egypt when he tried to

(a) abolish slavery.
(b) unify Upper and Lower Egypt.
(c) establish monotheism.
(d) none of the above

(c) p. 14

1.-.25: The Egyptian god Osiris was believed to

(a) hold up the heavens.
(b) judge the dead.
(c) live on Mount Ararat.
(d) be the god of evil.

(b) p. 15

1.-.26: The Rosetta Stone provided the key to understanding

(a) Linear A.
(b) Egyptian hieroglyphics.
(c) early Jewish history.
(d) cuneiform.

(b) p. 15

1.-.27: Egyptian society was

(a) without a slave class.
(b) relatively egalitarian.
(c) wholly agricultural.
(d) divided into classes.

(d) p. 16

1.-.28: The "ka" was important in Egypt because

(a) it was a valuable cash crop in the Nile delta.
(b) it left the body at death but could return at any time.
(c) it provided the justification for monarchical rule.
(d) it was a means of writing which rendered hieroglyphics understandable.

(d) p. 15

1.-.29: The Book of the Dead contained information about

(a) the epic of Gilgamesh.
(b) how to translate heiroglyphics.
(c) Egyptian religious beliefs.
(d) the first five books of the Hebrew scripture.

(c) p. 15

1.-.30: The word "Semitic" refers

(a) only to Jews.
(b) a family of languages used by Greeks and Romans.
(c) a family of languages used by Akkadians and Hebrews.
(d) only to Egyptians.

(a) p. 17

1.-.31: The city of Carthage was founded by the

(a) Philistines.
(b) Phoenicians.
(c) Minoans.
(d) "Sea-peoples."

(b) p. 18

1.-.32: The alphabet used by most Western civilizations was derived from that used by the

(a) Akkadians.
(b) Assyrians.
(c) Anatolians.
(d) Phoenicians.

(d) p. 18

1.-.33: The first people to set down their history in books were the

(a) Hebrews.
(b) Egyptians.
(c) Mycenaeans.
(d) Persians.

(a) p. 18

1.-.34: Archaeological evidence indicates that the story set forth in the Bible is

(a) largely mythical.
(b) a valuable historical source.
(c) impossible to substantiate.
(d) linked to Minoan culture.

(b) p. 19

1.-.35: The religion of the Hebrew people was essentially

(a) polytheistic.
(b) animistic.
(c) anthropomorphic.
(d) monotheistic.

(d) p. 19

1.-.36: The Hebrews endured a long period of captivity at the hands of the

(a) Amorites.
(b) Medes.
(c) Hurrians.
(d) Babylonians.

(d) p. 19

1.-.37: The prophets warned their fellow Hebrews of the religious influence of the

(a) Canaanites.
(b) Assyrians.
(c) Hittites.
(d) Lydians.

(a) p. 19

1.-.38: The social structure and laws of the ancient Hebrews permitted

(a) slaves.
(b) polygamy.
(c) neither of the above.
(d) both of the above.

(c) p. 20

1.-.39: Which of the following statements about Minoan civilization is NOT true?

(a) It was based on maritime trade.
(b) Women held near equal status with men.
(c) Its language, Linear A, was a Greek dialect.
(d) It was excavated by Sir Arthur Evans.

(c) p. 20

1.-.40: "Egg-shell" pottery, bare-breasted goddesses, and ritual games of bull jumping were characteristics of this civilization.

(a) Minoan.
(b) Trojan.
(c) Mycenaean.
(d) Lydian.

(a) pp. 20-21

1.-.41: Mycenaean culture was greatly influenced by that found

(a) among the Anatolians.
(b) in North Africa.
(c) on the island of Crete.
(d) in Iran.

(c) p. 22

1.-.42: The language of the script known as Linear B was

(a) Semitic.
(b) of Akkadian origin.
(c) early Greek.
(d) Egyptian.

(c) p. 22

1.-.43: During the Trojan War, Troy was attacked by the forces of

(a) the Egyptian pharaoh.
(b) the Cretans.
(c) the Hittites.
(d) the Mycenaean king Agamemnon.

(d) p. 23

1.-.44: For literature, the most important episode in the period 1400 to 1100 B.C was

(a) the discovery of Linear A.
(b) the Trojan War.
(c) the Mycenaean occupation of Greece.
(d) the creation of the Assyrian Empire.

(b) p. 23

1.-.45: Mycenaean civilization was replaced by a "dark age" which saw these people invade and settle extensive areas of Greece.

(a) Achaeans
(b) Dorians
(c) Celts
(d) Phrygians

(b) p. 24

1.-.46: Both the "Iliad" and the "Odyssey" traditionally are attributed to

(a) Priam.
(b) Hesiod.

(c) Hector.
(d) Homer.

(d) p. 24

1.-.47: Cuneiform allows scholars access to Sumerian history
(True) p. 10

1.-.48: Lascaux and Altamira provide excellent evidence of Paleolithic art. (True) p. 6

1.-.49: At Jericho, archeologists have determined by radio-carbon dating that the town is 78,000 years old. (False) p. 7.

1.-.50: A hydraulic society, such as Sumer, was one primarily focused around mechanization and industry. (False) p. 10

1.-.51: Mesopotamian rulers were considered living gods on earth. (False) pp. 12-13

1.-.52: For Egyptians, the ka was the indestructible vital principle of each person. (True) p. 15

1.-.53: In Egyptian society, women could not own land, transact business, or succeed to the throne. (False) p. 18

1.-.54: Queen Nefertiti ruled in Babylon. (False) p. 16

1.-.55: The period when Homer composed the "Iliad" and the "Odyssey" is called the "golden age." (False) p. 24

1.-.56: What do historians mean when they use the word "civilization," and how do they identify the first civilizations?

1.-.57: How do historians distinguish between "prehistory" and early history, and what does the remains of written records have to do with the distinction?

1.-.58: Write an essay comparing ancient Mesopotamia and Egypt, addressing the topics of politics, society, and religion.

1.-.59: Show how archeological discoveries have influenced our views of Minoan and Mycenaean civilizations

1.-.60: Who was Homer, and what contributions did he make to ancient and modern civilization?

1.-.61: What were the roles of towns, the countryside, and river systems in early civilizations? Give specific examples.

1.-.62: Historical writings, archeological discoveries, and changes in place names, all give us information on ancient civilizations. Write an essay providing specific examples of each.

1.-.63: "Whoever controls history and how it is written, controls the past, and who controls the past controls the present."

Write an essay commenting on that statement, drawing examples from the history of the first civilzations, as we know them.

1.-.64: Write an essay comparing and contrasting the religious systems of the major civilizations discussed in this chapter, using examples to emphasize the concepts of monotheism and polytheism.

TEST ITEM FILE

CHAPTER 2: THE GREEKS

2.-.1: Modern Western societies often feel an affinity for ancient Greek civilization because of the Greeks'

(a) artistic ideals.
(b) political institutions.
(c) sense of history.
(d) all of the above.

(d) p. 26

2.-.2: Government in the poleis of Greece in their early stage of development was in the hands of

(a) a priestly class.
(b) the prominent men.
(c) an assembly of the people.
(d) tyrants.

(b) p. 27

2.-.3: Which of the following was NOT a factor leading the Greeks to undertake large-scale colonial expansion?

(a) overpopulation
(b) internal strife
(c) the search for trade
(d) the pressure of barbarians

(b) p. 29

2.-.4: The two most significant Greek poleis, whose rivalry led to the Peloponnesian Wars, were

(a) Thebes and Sparta.
(b) Persia and Athens.
(c) Syracuse and Marathon.
(d) Sparta and Athens.

(d) p. 34

2.-.5: The primary function of the helots in Spartan society was

(a) agricultural labor.
(b) religious.
(c) judicial.
(d) military.

(a) p. 29

2.-.6: Lycurgus was said to have

(a) been the first playwright of Athens.
(b) written the Sparta constitution.
(c) founded the Delian League.
(d) established the Olympic games.

(b) p. 29

2.-.7: The Athenian Draco was appointed to

(a) set down the law.
(b) command the Greeks at Marathon.
(c) serve as the city's tyrant.
(d) none of the above

(a) p. 38

2.-.8: Which of the following was NOT a reform of Solon?

(a) the fostering of commerce
(b) encouragement of aliens to settle in Athens
(c) establishment of the Council of Four Hundred
(d) opening the highest public offices to all male citizens

(d) p. 30

2.-.9: He governed many years as the "tyrant" of Athens

(a) Solon
(b) Draco
(c) Pisistratus
(d) Leonidas

(c) p. 39

2.-.10: He reorganized the political structure of Athens to create a near democracy.

(a) Pericles
(b) Cleon
(c) Cleisthenes
(d) Alcibiades

(c) p. 30

2.-.11: In Greek society slavery was

(a) limited to agricultural workers.
(b) generally viewed as a distasteful system.
(c) ended as a consequence of the reforms of Solon.

(d) justified by appealing to economic necessity.

(d) p. 31

2.-.12: Which of the following statements regarding the status of Greek women is NOT true?

(a) They enjoyed great political and legal rights.
(b) Their role was defined by class.
(c) Some women took part in business.
(d) Some Greek gods were female.

(a) p. 31

2.-.13: The concept of the universe as a battleground for the forces of good and evil was found in

(a) Zoroastrianism.
(b) the teachings of Plato.
(c) the teachings of the Sophists.
(d) the cult of Dionysius.

(a) p. 32

2.-.14: The initial victory of the Athenians over the Persians was won at

(a) Plataea.
(b) Marathon.
(c) Issus.
(d) the Dardanelles.

(b) p. 33

2.-.15: The Athenian statesman who advocated that his fellow citizens build a naval force to oppose the Persians was
(a) Nicias.
(b) Isocrates.
(c) Themistocles.
(d) Cleisthenes.

(c) p. 33

2.-.16: During its "Golden Age" the leading statesman of Athens was

(a) Themistocles.
(b) Alcibiades.
(c) Pericles..
(d) Cleon.

(c) p. 35

2.-.17: The wealth of the Delian League was used by Pericles to beautify the city of Athens, which included the construction of

(a) the Persepolis.
(b) the theater at Epidaurus.
(c) the Parthenon.
(d) the Winged Victory of Samothrace.

(c) pp. 34, 47

2.-.18: Athens suffered a major defeat in the Peloponnesian war as a consequence of

(a) Philip of Macedon's intervention.
(b) the campaign in Sicily.
(c) the Spartan occupation of Athens in 431 B.C.
(d) the Trojan horse.

(b) p. 35

2.-.19: Following the Peloponnesian War, this polis sought to become the master of Greece

(a) Corinth.
(b) Sparta.
(c) Syracuse.
(d) Athens.

(b) p. 36

2.-.20: The creation of Macedonian political and military power was the great achievement of

(a) Cyrus.
(b) Philip II.
(c) Antigonus.
(d) Seleucus I.

(b) p. 38

2.-.21: Which of the following places were NOT conquered by Alexander the Great?

(a) modern-day Pakistan.
(b) Carthage.
(c) Egypt.
(d) Babylon.

(b) pp. 38, 39

2.-.22: On his death, Alexander's empire passed into the hands of his

(a) son by his Persian wife.
(b) mother.
(c) half-brother..
(d) generals.

(d) p. 39

2.-.23: The period between the reign of Alexander the Great and the first Roman emperor is generally known as the

(a) Athenian period.
(b) Macedonian period.
(c) Hellenistic period.
(d) Persian period.

(c) p 39

2.-.24: After Alexander the Great's death, three dynasties emerged, including all of the following EXCEPT the

(a) Ptolemies.
(b) Antigonids.
(c) Sassanids.
(d) Seleucids.

(c) p. 39

2.-.25: Which of the following was NOT an economic problem for the heirs of Alexander the Great?

(a) rising inflation
(b) poor harvests
(c) Persian gold
(d) warfare

(b) p. 56

2.-.26: Demeter, who was worshipped at Eleusis, was the goddess of

(a) love.
(b) the polis of Athens.
(c) the hearth.
(d) fertility.

(d) p. 42

2.-.27: Which of the following is NOT considered one of the great Greek tragedians?

(a) Aeschylus
(b) Sophocles
(c) Thucydides
(d) Euripedes

(c) pp. 42, 43

2.-.28: The story of Oedipus and his tragic fate was told in the play of

(a) Aristophanes.

(b) Sophocles.
(c) Menander.
(d) Euripides.

(b) p. 42

2.-.29: Called the "father of history," he wrote of the great conflict between the Greeks and Persia.

(a) Xenophon
(b) Herodotus
(c) Cadmus
(d) Thucydides

(b) p. 44

2.-.30: A historian of the Peloponnesian wars, this Greek author reconstructed the funeral oration of Pericles.

(a) Xenophon
(b) Polybius
(c) Herodotus
(d) Thucydides

(d) p. 44

2.-.31: His followers sought to explain the universe in mathematical terms.

(a) Hippocrates
(b) Plato
(c) Pythagoras
(d) Socrates

(c) p. 45

2.-.32: The Hellenistic scientist Eratosthenes

(a) argued that all matter was composed of "atoms."
(b) measured quite accurately the circumference of the earth.
(c) advanced the so-called "Theory of Ideas."
(d) invented a steam engine.

(b) p. 45

2.-.33: His method of seeking the truth was a never-ending process of questions and answers.

(a) Epicurus
(b) Socrates
(c) Polybius
(d) Phidias

(b) p. 45

2.-.34: He held that the world we experience with our bodily senses is not actually the "true world" of Ideas.

(a) Plato
(b) Aristotle
(c) Epicurus
(d) Zeno

(a) p. 46

2.-.35: This advanced the vision of an ideal state governed by a "guardian class" and a philosopher-king.

(a) the cult of Zeus
(b) The Republic
(c) The Clouds
(d) Sophism

(b) p. 46

2.-.36: The first to use scientific methods, he advocated the avoidance of excess in all things

(a) Socrates
(b) Plato
(c) Pythagorus
(d) Aristotle

(d) p. 46

2.-.37: In Greek architecture, the orders of columns included all but

(a) Corinthian.
(b) Doric.
(c) Gothic.
(d) Ionic.

(c) p. 48

2.-.38: The Laocoon is a famed Hellenistic

(a) oracle on the island of Melos.
(b) comedy by Aeschylus.
(c) a statue depicting terror.
(d) temple dedicated to Zeus.

(c) p. 49

2.-.39: In contrast to many Greek poleis, Sparta long retained the office of king. (True) p. 29

2.-.40: The tyrant Pisistratus came to power in Athens as a leader of the lower class. (True) p. 30

2.-.41: The word "draconian" has a root referring to a gentle Athenian law-giver. (False) p. 30

2.-.42: Philip II of Macedon was slain because he opposed the idea of attempting the conquest of the Persian Empire. (False) p. 38

2.-.43: In the Greek mind, hubris --arrogance-- was the worst of all the sins of man. (True) p. 42

2.-.44: Plato's Republic advocated democracy as the ideal state. (False) p. 46

2.-.45: Write an essay describing parts of our modern culture which stem from ancient Greek ideas.

2.-.46: The polis and the concepts of "citizenship" and "colony" were developed by the Greeks. Describe each of them, giving specific examples.

2.-.47: Compare and contrast the political organization of Sparta and Athens, noting the theoretical and practical limits of their very different approaches to the ideals of government.

2.-.49: Write an essay on the major Greek dramatists, Aristophanes, and Sophocles, noting how the elements of tragedy and comedy are exhibited in their works.

2.-.50: Write an essay describing the status of women in ancient Greece and the implicit criticism of that situation in the great works of Greek culture.

TEST ITEM FILE

CHAPTER 3: THE ROMANS

3.-.1: The physical geography of Italy is somewhat more favorable than that of Greece because

(a) the city of Rome is directly on the sea coast.
(b) the plains are larger and more fertile.
(c) Italy is considerably smaller than Greece.
(d) Italy has a Mediterranean climate.

(b) p. 51

3.-.2: For nearly a century the people of Rome were ruled by the

(a) Gauls.
(b) Carthaginians.
(c) Samnites.
(d) Etruscans.

(d) p. 52

3.-.3: With the establishment of the Roman Republic in 509 B.C executive power was placed in the hands of the

(a) king.
(b) aediles.
(c) tribunes.
(d) consuls.

(d) p. 52

3.-.4: In the early Republic, Roman political and social power was held by the

(a) plebians.
(b) equites.
(c) patricians.
(d) urban proletariat.

(c) p. 52

3.-.5: In the early Roman Republic, upper-class women were able to

(a) participate in business.
(b) hold property.
(c) practice contraception and abortion.
(d) all of the above.

(c) p. 53

3.-.6: The leading power of the Senatus Populusque Romanorum (SPQR), the political emblem of Rome, was the

(a) consuls.
(b) plebians.
(c) Senate.
(d) Assembly.

(c) p. 52

3.-.7: In the Punic Wars, the Romans fought and finally defeated the armies of

(a) the Gauls.
(b) the Etruscans.
(c) Carthage.
(d) Macedon.

(c) p. 54

3.-.8: <u>Latifundia</u> were

(a) state monopolies under the administration of the Senate.
(b) settlements of Germans who served as mercenaries in Rome's armies.
(c) large mixed farms or cattle ranches worked by slaves.
(d) colonies founded by Romans in their overseas provinces.

(c) p. 56

3.-.9: Which of the following was NOT a reform sought by the Grachi brothers?

(a) to open certain judicial posts to men of the <u>equites</u> class
(b) to provide land for the landless small farmers of Italy
(c) to abolish the office of consul
(d) to provide cheap grain for the urban poor

(c) p. 56

3.-.10: The first Roman to utilize a "personal" army to establish himself and to dominate the Senate and the political life of the Republic was

(a) Marius.
(b) Caligula.
(c) Pompey the Great.
(d) Cicero.

(a) p. 56

3.-.11: A gladiator, he led a great slave rebellion against the Republic.

(a) Jugurtha
(b) Spartacus
(c) Mithridates
(d) Scipio

(b) p. 56

3.-.12: Which of the following was NOT a member of the First Triumvirate?

(a) Pompey the Great
(b) Julius Caesar
(c) Lepidus
(d) Crassus

(c) p. 57

3.-.13: Julius Caesar initially built his reputation as a great military leader through his conquest of

(a) Spain.
(b) England.
(c) Parthia.
(d) Gaul.

(d) p. 57

3.-.14: Julius Caesar was slain by

(a) leaders of the urban poor who feared his monarchial ambitions.
(b) senators who claimed they were protecting the Republic.
(c) druids angered at his refusal to grant them citizenship.
(d) agents of the Egyptian queen, Cleopatra.

(b) p. 58

3.-.15: His victory over Mark Antony and Cleopatra made him sole master of the Roman world.

(a) Lepidus
(b) Octavian
(c) Cicero
(d) Brutus

(b) p. 58

3.-.16: Which of the following was NOT an achievement of Augustus (Octavian) during the years he ruled the Roman Empire?

(a) reduction of the size of the Senate
(b) extensive urban renewal in the city of Rome
(c) extension of the Roman frontier beyond the Rhine River
(d) the enactment of social laws to strengthen and enlarge families

(c) p. 59

3.-.17: At Teutoburger Forest, Arminius gave the Romans evidence of the great danger presented by

(a) rebellious generals.
(b) the Persian Empire.
(c) the Germans.
(d) the Huns.

(c) p. 59

3.-.18: The crucifixion of Christ took place while this man ruled as emperor.

(a) Julius Caesar
(b) Tiberius
(c) Nero
(d) Marcus Aurelius

(b) p. 60

3.-.19: While Nero sat on the imperial throne, serious rebellions against Rome broke out in

(a) Ireland and Greece.
(b) Britain and Judea.
(c) Egypt and Sicily.
(d) Carthage and Macedon.

(b) p. 60

3.-.20: Following the death of the Emperor Nero

(a) his mother Agrippina briefly ruled the Roman Empire.
(b) the Senate was able to select Vespasian as his successor.
(c) four military men occupied the throne in rapid succession.
(d) the Republic was restored for five years.

(c) p. 61

3.-.21: Which of the following statements regarding the status of women in the later Roman Empire is NOT true?

(a) They found it difficult to cross class barriers.
(b) Many women were actively engaged in business.
(c) The state viewed the bearing of male children their primary role.
(d) They enjoyed much greater freedom than did women of Greece.

(a) p. 63

3.-.22: Which of the following contributd to the decline in population of the Roman Empire?

(a) barbarian raids
(b) plague
(c) economic decline
(d) all of the above

(d) p. 64

3.-.23: The end of the "Pax Romana" and the beginning of the "decline" of the Roman Empire is usually associated with the death of the emperor

(a) Vespasian.
(b) Hadrian.
(c) Marcus Aurelius.
(d) Trajan.

(c) p. 64

3.-.24: The system of rule known as the tetrarchy was introduced by

(a) Septimius Severus.
(b) Theodosius the Great.
(c) Diocletian.
(d) Caracalla.

(c) p. 65

3.-.25: The emperor Diocletian

(a) adopted the trappings of an oriental monarch.
(b) moved the capital from Rome to the Rhine frontier.
(c) combined the functions of the civil and military officials.
(d) reduced the size of the Roman army.

(a) p. 66

3.-.26: Reflecting attitudes of his own age, the eighteenth-century historian Edward Gibbon blamed Rome's decline on

(a) the Germans.
(b) wide-spread plague.
(c) Christianity.
(d) ineffective leadership.

(c) p. 66

3.-.27: Instead of blaming the barbarian invasions, Henri Pirenne argued that the decline of the Roman Empire was the result of

(a) civil wars.
(b) lead poisoning.
(c) slavery.
(d) Arab activity.

(d) p. 67

3.-.28: The Pontifex Maximus acted as Rome's

(a) chief judicial official.
(b) high priest.
(c) commander of the army.
(d) first consul.

(b) p. 67

3.-.29: He was held to have been the greatest writer of Latin prose

(a) Catullus.
(b) Cicero.
(c) Fabius Pictor.
(d) Galen.

(b) p. 68

3.-.30: He praised the rugged Germans and criticized the pursuit of luxury by the Romans.

(a) Ovid
(b) Commodus
(c) Tacitus
(d) Lucretius

(c) p. 70

3.-.31: Which of the following was NOT a poet in the Roman Empire?

(a) Vergil
(b) Euclid
(c) Catullus
(d) Horace

(b) p. 68

3.-.32: The earliest Roman legal code was the

(a) Satyricon.
(b) Twelve Tables.
(c) Metamorphoses.
(d) Annales.

(b) p. 70

3.-.33: The first Roman province established in Asia Minor was Pergamum. (True) p. 54

3.-.34: The *equites* class was drawn from the urban poor. (False) p. 56

3.-.35: The final limit of Roman conquest to the North in Europe was the frontier of the Rhine River. (True) p. 61

3.-.36: Mount Vesuvius erupted, destroying Pompeii. (True) p. 62

3.-.37: Hadrian's Wall marked the border between Roman Britain and Scotland. (True) p. 63

3.-.38: The last centuries of the Roman Empire saw a marked population decline. (True) p. 64

3.-.39: Gibbon was a wealthy Roman who predicted the fall of the Empire. (False) p. 66

3.-.40: Roman law recognized the legal rights of citizens, but also of slaves. (True) p. 70

3.-.41: Ovid and Catullus wrote poetry on the art of love. (True) pp. 68-69

3.-.42: The Satyricon was a major Roman work dealing with the art of warfare. (False) p. 68

3.-.43: The Roman Galen was for centuries viewed as a major authority in the field of medicine. (True) p. 70

3.-.44: Write an essay describing the government of the Roman Republic, and how it dealt with social and political crises.

3.-.45: Julius Caesar was a pivot around which the history of Rome developed. Select two other Roman leaders and describe their achievements.

3.-.46: Write an essay describing the Pax Romana, indicating the degree to which it was indeed peaceful, and the degree to which it was dependent upon military power.

3.-.47: The rise and fall of the Roman Empire is one of the great epics of our history. Write an essay analyzing the reasons for both its rise and its ultimate decline.

3.-.48: "The Greeks passed to us their sense of culture, but the Romans passed us their sense of power." Respond to that statement, noting the major contributions of both the Greeks and the Romans to our modern civilization.

3.-.49: Latin and Greek were both languages used in the Roman Empire. Write an essay describing the importance of each.

3.-.50: Describe the daily life in Rome during the height of the Empire, contrasting the lives of the rich and the poor.

TEST ITEM FILE

CHAPTER 4

4.-.1: The work of Hero of Alexandria and Vitruvius revealed the potential of the Greeks and Romans in the area of

(a) maritime exploration.
(b) applied science.
(c) administration.
(d) law.

(b) p. 73

4.-.2: Which of the following is NOT a possible explanation for the failure of the Romans to develop the applied sciences?

(a) a disdain for "idle speculation" on the part of the ruling class
(b) the extensive use of slave labor
(c) the lack of an extensive consumer market
(d) great optimism in man's ability to work out his own future

(d) p. 74

4.-.3: Romans developed the practice of sacrificing bulls to Cybele in order to

(a) show the power of woman over a mighty beast.
(b) permit an initiate to be bathed in its blood.
(c) provide food for the Roman masses .
(d) demonstrate the inadequacy of monotheism.

(b) pp. 74, 75

4.-.4: Religious cults such as those of Isis, Cybele, and Mithra had in common all but

(a) the promise of a happy afterlife.
(b) long periods of initiation.
(c) the concept of the individual's soul uniting with that of a saviour.
(d) a strong appeal to the educated classes.

(d) p. 75

4.-.5: Which of the following philosophies taught of the eventual union of man's soul with "the One"?

(a) Stoicism
(b) Epicureanism
(c) Neoplatonism
(d) Hedonism

(c) p. 75

4.-.6: Most Romans acknowledged the great power of planets, comets, and magic because of their belief in

(a) Christianity.
(b) astronomy.
(c) astrology.
(d) science.

(c) p. 74

4.-.7: The so-called Dead Sea Scrolls have revealed much about the

(a) Essenes.
(b) Hasmoneans.
(c) Pharisees.
(d) sanhedrin.

(a) p. 77

4.-.8: The Zealots were

(a) a small sect of Jews who lived in monastic communes.
(b) scribes attached to the Temple in Jerusalem.
(c) Jewish resistors seeking to expel the Romans from Judah.
(d) Jewish scholars committed to private study.

(c) p. 78

4.-.9: Paul is well known as the man who

(a) wrote the last and most comprehensive of the four gospels.
(b) led the Jewish rebellion against Rome which led to the destruction of the Temple.
(c) converted from a persecutor of Christians to a Christian himself.
(d) argued that only the followers of Jewish law could become Christians.

(c) pp. 78, 79

4.-.10: Which of the following statements about Paul is NOT true?

(a) He believed Christianity was for Gentiles as well as Jews.
(b) He had initially persecuted the Christians.
(c) As Christ's closest companion, he believed himself his successor.
(d) He was martyred in Rome during the persecutions of Nero.

(c) p. 79

4.-.11: The question of how the state should deal with Christians was discussed in his letters with the Emperor Trajan.

(a) Pliny the Younger
(b) Ambrose of Milan
(c) St. Jerome

(d) St. Augustine

(a) p. 81

4.-.12: In A.D. 313 the Edict of Milan

(a) declared Arianism a heresy.
(b) ended the Donatist conflict.
(c) granted Christians toleration.
(d) outlawed pagan religious practices.

(c) p. 81

4.-.13: Christianity was made the official religion of the Roman state by Emperor

(a) Julian the Apostate.
(b) Constantine.
(c) Diocletian.
(d) Theodosius I.

(d) p. 82

4.-.14: The concept of "apostolic succession" was the basis of the spiritual authority of

(a) abbots of monasteries.
(b) church fathers.
(c) bishops.
(d) prophets.

(c) p. 83

4.-.15: The claim of the bishop of Rome to supremacy in the Christian Church is based on the

(a) Nicene Creed.
(b) Petrine theory.
(c) doctrine of Caesaropapism.
(d) Edict of Milan.

(b) p. 83

4.-.16: His courage helped save the city of Rome from attack by Attila the Hun.

(a) Arius
(b) St. Benedict of Nursia
(c) Pope Leo the Great
(d) Athanasius

(c) p. 83

4.-.17: He translated the Old and New Testaments from Greek into Latin.

(a) St. Basil

(b) Tertullian
(c) St. Augustine
(d) Jerome

(d) p. 83

4.-.18: Christian monasticism was first seen in

(a) Egypt.
(b) southern Italy and Gaul.
(c) Greece.
(d) Spain.

(a) p. 84

4.-.19: One of the earliest "rules" governing the lives of monks was drawn up by

(a) Ambrose of Milan.
(b) Anthony.
(c) Pelagius.
(d) Constantine the Great.

(b) p. 84

4.-.20: Founder of the great monastery of Monte Cassino, he wrote the monastic rule that became the most important in Western Europe.

(a) Pope Leo the Great.
(b) St. Benedict.
(c) Mani.
(d) St. Paul.

(b) pp. 84, 85

4.-.21: Which of the following was NOT one of the seven sacraments?

(a) baptism
(b) extreme unction
(c) the Eucharist
(d) good works

(d) p. 86

4.-.22: The early Christian church was challenged by heresies, including

(a) Gnosticism.
(b) Manichaean beliefs.
(c) Arianism.
(d) all of the above.

(d) p. 86

4.-.23: They believed that the physical world is evil and that the god of the Old Testament, who created it, was a fiend.

(a) believers in Gnosticism
(b) the Essenes
(c) the Nestorians
(d) the Monophysites

(a) p. 86

4.-.24: The ancient concept of a god of light and goodness and a god of evil and darkness was revived in

(a) Pelagianism.
(b) Manichaeanism.
(c) Julian the Apostate's writings.
(d) The City of God.

(b) p. 86

4.-.25: Who denied the equality "in essence" of God the Son to God the Father?

(a) St. Jerome
(b) the Donatists
(c) Arius
(d) Athanasius

(c) p. 86

4.-.26: To settle the quarrel over the nature of Christ, Constantine called a council which developed

(a) the Chalcedon decision.
(b) the Nicene Creed.
(c) Manichaean doctrine.
(d) the Edict of Milan.

(b) p. 87

4.-.27: The "regular" were distinguished from the "secular" clergy because

(a) the regular clergy lived by a monastic rule.
(b) the secular clergy were heretics.
(c) the regular clergy included women.
(d) the regular clergy received cash salaries.

(a) p. 84

4.-.28: The Eucharist is the central sacrament of Christianity because

(a) every Christian partakes only once in a lifetime.
(b) it stems from Jesus's last supper with his disciples.
(c) it was based on Roman mythology.

(d) it was begun by the first pope in Rome.

(b) p. 85

4.-.29: St. Augustine's The City of God was written in response to the

(a) sack of Rome in A.D. 410.
(b) Edict of Milan.
(c) Council of Nicaea.
(d) Vulgate Latin Bible.

(a) p. 89

4.-.30: The struggle between St. Augustine and Pelagius centered on the issue of

(a) dualism.
(b) free will and predestination.
(c) the Trinity.
(d) the supremacy of the papacy.

(b) p. 90

4.-.31: The cult of Mithra was particularly popular with Roman soldiers. (True) p. 75

4.-.32: Greek thought had little influence among the Jewish peoples. (False) pp. 76, 77

4.-.33: The Stoic philosophers wrote of the "Teacher of Righteousness.6 (False) p. 77

4.-.34: Women had little to do with spreading the words of Jesus. (False) p. 78

4.-.35: The Emperor Julian the Apostate sought to revive the philosophies and gods of old within the Roman Empire. (True) p. 82

4.-.36: The basic rule of monasticism for the Eastern Christian Church was written by St. Basil. (True) p. 84

4.-.37: The decision of the Council at Chalcedon supported monophysitism. (False) p. 87

4.-.38: St. Augustine's Confessions dealt with the rise of the papacy in the first two centuries of the Christian Church. (False) p. 89

4.-.39: Christianity triumphed in the Roman Empire because it offered a new and believable spiritual promise, yet preserved certain familiar elements. (True) p. 91

4.-.40: What elements contributed to the spread of Christianity throughout the Roman world? Consider both the problems of the Roman culture and the attractive aspects of the new faith.

4.-.41: Describe how Rome ruled Judea in the first centuries B.C. and A.D., and the interactions between the Roman and Hebrew civilization.

4.-.42: Write an essay describing the Sadducees, Pharisees, Zealots, and Essenes in Judea, noting the differences between them.

4.-.43: What was the relationship between the ideas of Judaism and Christianity during the first century A.D.? Why was there conflict between them?

4.-.44: Name the seven sacraments of the traditional Christian Church in the West, and describe their functions.

4.-.45: Write an essay describing the most important teachings of Jesus, and consider how they were developed by St. Augustine.

4.-.46: Discuss the religious ideas of Constantine the Great and the role he played in the development of Christianity in the Roman Empire.

4.-.47: Write an essay considering the importance of the religious developments in the Roman Empire for the role of women, noting both the influence of Christianity and those of the mystery cults.

4.-.48: Describe the organizational development of the early Christian church, and indicate the importance of monasteries for that development.

4.-.49: How did heresy threaten the unity of the Christian church in Roman times, and how was heresy dealt with by Roman leaders?

4.-.50: Compare and contrast the religious beliefs and practices of the Jews and the Christians during the Roman Empire.

TEST ITEM FILE

CHAPTER 5: THE EARLY MIDDLE AGES IN WESTERN EUROPE

5.-.1: Which of the following general statements about the early Middle Ages is NOT true?

(a) Marked technological advances in certain specific areas occurred.
(b) The Christian Church maintained the most consistent authority.
(c) The Germanic invaders were hostile to all aspects of Roman civilization.
(d) The authors of the primary sources for the period were largely antagonistic to the Germans.

(c) p. 95

5.-.2: Which of the following terms do contemporary historians prefer to call the period 500 to 1000 A.D.?

(a) Dark Ages
(b) early Middle Ages
(c) late antiquity
(d) early modern Europe

(b) p. 94

5.-.3: In A.D. 410 the city of Rome was sacked by the forces of
(a) Alaric the Visigoth.
(b) Odovacar the Hun.
(c) Theodoric the Ostrogoth.
(d) Clovis the Frank.

(a) p. 96

5.-.4: At Adrianople in A.D. 378 Emperor Valens was defeated and slain by the

(a) Huns.
(b) Visigoths.
(c) Anglo-Saxons.
(d) Franks.

(b) p. 96

5.-.5: The Avars, Bulgars, and Magyars were all

(a) converted to the Islamic faith.
(b) unable to establish permanent states.
(c) nomadic horsemen from central Asia.
(d) destroyed by the armies of Charlemagne.

(c) p. 97

5.-.6: The "end" of the Roman Empire in the West was marked by the

(a) sacking of Rome by the Vandals.
(b) dethroning of Emperor Romulus Augustulus by Odovacar.
(c) coronation of the Frankish monarch Charles the Great.
(d) seizure of Italy by Theodoric the Ostrogoth.

(b) p. 96

5.-.7: By the eighth century real political power in the Frankish kingdom was in the hands of the

(a) bishops.
(b) mayors of the palace.
(c) regular clergy.
(d) rois faineants.

(b) p. 99

5.-.8: At Poitiers in A.D. 732 Charles Martel, "the Hammer," defeated an invading force of

(a) Vikings.
(b) Byzantines
(c) Arabs.
(d) Avars.

(c) p. 98

5.-.9: The first monarch of the Carolingian dynasty was

(a) Merevig (Merovech).
(b) Pepin the Short.
(c) Clovis.
(d) Charles Martel.

(b) p. 98

5.-.10: Soon after the death of Theodoric the Ostrogoth in A.D. 526, Italy and North Africa were conquered by the armies of

(a) Charlemagne.
(b) Islam.
(c) Justinian.
(d) the Northmen.

(c) p. 98

5.-.11: The "Donation of Pepin" resulted in the

(a) Frankish king submitting to the authority of the pope.
(b) establishment of the first monastery in France.
(c) recognition of the Frankish king as "emperor of the Roman people."

(d) granting of territories in central Italy to the papac.y

(d) p. 99

5.-.12: The epic poem "Le Chanson de Roland" tells of the exploits of troops of Charlemagne in

(a) the lands east of the Rhine.
(b) Spain.
(c) Italy.
(d) his war with the Avars.

(b) p. 100

5.-.13: Charlemagne sought to revive the Roman Empire in the West by

(a) attacking Constantinople.
(b) building a new capital in Paris.
(c) accepting the crown as "Roman Emperor Carolus Augustus."
(d) establishing an elaborate system of resident civil servants.

(c) p. 100

5.-.14: The Strasbourg Oaths of A.D. 842 were of historical interest because they

(a) represented a firm papal-imperial alliance.
(b) were administered in two languages, early French and early Germanic.
(c) established the title of "Holy Roman Emperor."
(d) marked the first alliance between a French and English monarch.

(b) p. 101

5.-.15: Which of the following is a possible explanation for the overseas expansion of the Northmen?

(a) search for booty
(b) overpopulation at home
(c) desire to find wives
(d) all of the above

(d) p. 102

5.-.16: Which of the following regions did NOT see the establishment of permanent settlements by the Norsemen?

(a) Ireland
(b) England
(c) France
(d) Spain

(d) pp. 102, 103

5.-.17: By the middle of the tenth century his heirs ruled over all of England.

(a) William the Conqueror
(b) Louis the Pious
(c) Alfred the Great
(d) Edward the Confessor

(c) p. 103

5.-.18: This German emperor revived Charlemagne's title of "Roman Emperor."

(a) Otto I
(b) Canute
(c) Hugh Capet
(d) Louis the Child

(a) p. 104

5.-.19: The "Gefolge" or "comitatus" of the Germans is best defined as

(a) a priesthood.
(b) a war-band.
(c) the assembly of the people.
(d) the council of elders.

(b) p. 105

5.-.20: The Roman term "precarium," or land held temporarily by a vassal in return for service, referred to what in the Middle Ages was called a

(a) "beneficium" or "fief."
(b) "capitulare."
(c) "fidelis."
(d) "investiture."

(a) p. 105

5.-.21: Feudalism was a system which grew up to provide

(a) control of the countryside by absolute kings.
(b) some basic security for survival.
(c) a professional army and navy.
(d) papal control of imperial elections.

(a) p. 104

5.-.22: Which of the following was NOT one of the obligations involved in the lord-vassal relationship?

(a) aid
(b) wardship
(c) relief
(d) immunity

(d) p. 105

5.-.23: Strips, balks, and demesne are all terms associated with

(a) the feudal contract.
(b) the secular clergy.
(c) feudalism.
(d) manorialism.

(d) pp. 106, 107

5.-.24: During the early Middle Ages, which of the following was NOT a development in agricultural technique?

(a) three field rotation of crops
(b) horse-collar and shoes
(c) large teams of oxen called "coloni"
(d) heavy-wheeled plows

(c) p. 106

5.-.25: The Consolation of Philosophy, one of the most popular schoolbooks of the Middle Ages, was written by

(a) Alfred the Great.
(b) Sidonius Apollinaris.
(c) Isidore of Seville.
(d) Boethius.

(d) pp. 108, 109

5.-.26: Cassidorus made a significant contribution to the civilization during the early Middle Ages through

(a) his efforts to bring the Christian faith to Scandinavia.
(b) the emphasis he placed upon monks copying ancient literary works.
(c) his work The Ecclesiastical History of the English People.
(d) introduction of the windmill into western Europe.

(b) p. 109

5.-.27: The greatest of the cultivated writers of England in the early Middle Ages was

(a) the Venerable Bede.
(b) Fortunatus.
(c) Einhard.
(d) Robert of Clari.

(a) p. 146

5.-.28: A sort of encyclopedia, this work by Isidore of Seville was influential outside of Spain.

(a) Dialogues
(b) Etymologies
(c) hagiographies
(d) Ecclesiastical History

(b) p. 110

5.-.29: Brought to Charlemagne's palace school from England, he sought to expand the study of the seven liberal arts.

(a) Alcuin of York.
(b) Brian of Munster.
(c) Grendel.
(d) Odo of Bayeux.

(a) p. 110

5.-.30: "Beowulf" was

(a) the chief opponent of Charlemagne.
(b) a Germanic invader of the Roman Empire.
(c) a Swedish hero in an old English poem.
(d) the son of Grendel in Celtic mythology.

(c) p. 111

5.-.31: During the early Middle Ages Latin survived as the universal vernacular language of Europe. (False) p. 95

5.-.32: The Ostrogoths founded the most lasting political entity to arise from the ruins of the Roman Empire (False) p. 114

5.-.33: The term "rois faineants" (do-nothing kings) was applied to the last Merovingian kings. (True) p. 98

5.-.34: The Carolingian Empire was severely weakened by civil war waged among Charlemagne's grandsons. (True) p. 102

5.-.35: Tenants-in-chief held their fiefs directly from the king. (True) p. 106

5.-.36: Manorialism was a negotiated relationship between lord and vassal. (False) pp. 106, 107

5.-.37: Slavery disappeared in western Europe with Christianity's victory. (False) p. 109

5.-.38: An important historical source for the early Middle Ages is the correspondence of Pope Gregory the Great. (True) p. 109

5.-.39: Beowulf represents the most remarkable Old English literary survival (True) pp. 110, 111

5.-.40: Write an essay describing the barbarian invasions and how they changed the late Roman world. Consider not only political and geographic changes, but also the social, economic, and cultural life of the early Middle Ages.

5.-.41: What elements in the period of the early Middle Ages led some historians to refer to this as the "dark ages," and why do the authors of the text reject this term while using the term "Middle Ages"? Give examples of positive contributions to our civilization which date from this era.

5.-.42: The feudal system was by no means uniform throughout western Europe, but elements of it appear again and again, including the relationship of lord to vassal, and the agricultural organization known as the manor. Describe how the feudal system worked, and compare it to the political and economic system of the Roman Empire on the one hand, and that of political democracy and private enterprise today on the other.

5.-.43: Western Europe endured invasions by several groups during the early Middle Ages, including the Northmen, the Arabs, and the Magyars. Write an essay describing these invasions and the responses of western Europeans to them.

5.-.44: Among the Germanic tribes, the Franks were extremely successful. Write an essay describing their successes, and noting the role of Charlemagne.

5.-.45: Write an essay describing medieval slavery, and noting the role of the state and church in its theory and practice.

5.-.46: During the early Middle Ages, learning and literature was alive both in Latin and in vernacular languages. Write an essay describing both kinds of literature, citing specific examples.

5.-.47: Where did the Celtic cultures exist during the early Middle Ages, and what contributions did they make to Western Civilization as a whole?

5.-.48: "Our people shall be well taken care of and reduced to poverty by no one." Please identify the source of that quotation and discuss the importance of such a source to understand the lives of European men and women during the early Middle Ages.

5.-.49: Many of the medieval groups historians write about have been virtually forgotten by the general public, but the Vandals and the Huns sound somewhat more familiar. Write an essay analyzing how words in our language are related to their historical roots, and help to preserve (and sometimes distort) historical memory.

5.-.50: Write an essay set up as a debate on the following statement: "The early Middle Ages in Western Europe was indeed a dark age." Be sure your "debaters" give appropriate specific examples to support their claims.

TEST ITEM FILE

CHAPTER 6: BYZANTIUM AND ISLAM

6.-.1: The capital of the Eastern Roman Empire, today called Istanbul in Turkey, was also known as

(a) Constantinople.
(b) Byzantium.
(c) Tsargrad.
(d) all of the above.

(d) p. 115

6.-.2: The city of Constantinople was surrounded on three sides by bodies of water: which of the following was NOT one of them?

(a) Sea of Marmora
(b) the Aegean Sea
(c) the Golden Horn
(d) the Bosporos

(b) p. 115

6.-.3: The Code, Digests, Institutes, and Novels were set down during the reign of the emperor

(a) Heraclius.
(b) Leo the Isaurian.
(c) Justinian.
(d) Theodosius the Great.

(c) pp. 116, 117

6.-.4: The walls of Constantinople withstood all attackers until 1204, when the city fell to an army of

(a) Ottoman Turks.
(b) western crusaders.
(c) Mongols.
(d) Bulgars.

(b) p. 117

6.-.5: Byzantine diplomacy was characterized by

(a) complexity and intrigue.
(b) frequent use of marriage alliances.
(c) scorn for the western Europeans as "barbarians."
(d) all of the above.

(d) p. 118

6.-.6: Which of the following statements about the economic life of the Byzantine Empire is NOT true?

(a) The emperors maintained a firm monopoly on silk.
(b) A policy of debasement of coinage was frequently followed.
(c) The real basis of the economy was agriculture.
(d) Trade extended to lands as distant as India and Africa.

(b) pp. 118-120

6.-.7: Caesaropapism refers to the fact that in the Byzantine Empire

(a) religion played a less important role than in western Europe.
(b) all religious matters were in the hands of the patriarch.
(c) it was assumed that all individuals could achieve salvation.
(d) the emperors had authority over both church and state.

(d) p. 120

6.-.8: Monasticism in the Byzantine Empire

(a) adhered to the policy of strict poverty.
(b) never achieved the importance it did in the West.
(c) attracted many men as the direct route to salvation.
(d) was unpopular with a majority of the people.

(c) p. 121

6.-.9: The Iconoclastic Controversy centered on the question of the

(a) filioque clause.
(b) conversion of the Bulgars.
(c) veneration of images.
(d) statues of the pope.

(c) p. 121

6.-.10: The schism of 1054, which split the Roman Catholic and the Greek Orthodox churches, was occurred because of

(a) the iconoclastic controversy.
(b) the filioque controversy.
(c) cultural differences.
(d) all of the above.

(d) p. 121

6.-.11: An interesting view of the Byzantine court's impression of western Europeans is found in the Alexiad of

(a) Liudprand.

(b) Anna Comnena.
(c) Nicephorum Phocas.
(d) St. Basil.

(b) p. 121

6.-.12: The emperor Theophilis was legendary for his

(a) personal luxury.
(b) intellectual ability.
(c) acts of justice.
(d) ascetic piety.

(a) p. 117

6.-.13: The armies of Justinian reconquered briefly all of the following BUT

(a) southern Spain.
(b) North Africa.
(c) Italy.
(d) Gaul.

(d) p. 122

6.-.14: The nomisma was a

(a) Byzantine gold coin.
(b) Monophysite hermit.
(c) chapter of the Koran.
(d) holy man of the Sufi sect.

(a) p. 120

6.-.15: The Byzantine exarchate of Ravenna was extinguished by the

(a) Bulgars.
(b) Lombards.
(c) Avars.
(d) Arabs.

(b) p. 123

6.-.16: The victory of the Seljuk Turks at Manzikert led

(a) to their subsequent occupation of virtually all Asia Minor.
(b) to the cutting off of the Byzantine navy from the Mediterranean.
(c) almost immediately to the fall of Constantinople.
(d) to the destruction of the Crusader states of the Holy Land.

(a) p. 124

6.-.17: The alphabet still used by the Russians was invented by

(a) St. Cyril.
(b) Procopius.
(c) Vladimir the Wise.
(d) Anna Comnena.

(a) p. 124

6.-.18: The so-called "calling of the princes" spoken of in the Primary Chronicle resulted in the

(a) Slavs conversion to Christianity.
(b) settlement of Rurik and his followers in Russia.
(c) extensions of Byzantine power into the Balkans.
(d) First Crusade.

(b) pp. 124, 125

6.-.19: The principal city of medieval Russia was

(a) Odessa.
(b) Novgorod.
(c) Kiev.
(d) Smolensk.

(c) pp. 125, 126

6.-.20: To which of the following does Western Civilization credit as the primary preservers of the ancient Greek classics?

(a) Germans
(b) Bulgars
(c) Byzantines
(d) Mongols

(c) p. 126

6.-.21: Byzantine hagiographical works dealt with

(a) military tactics.
(b) the lives of the saints.
(c) financial administration.
(d) architecture.

(b) p. 127

6.-.22: Hagia Sophia was

(a) the sacred shrine of Muslims in Mecca.
(b) the most important monastic order of the Greek Orthodox Church.
(c) Justinian's great church in Constantinople.
(d) a site in Jerusalem sacred to Muslim, Jew, and Christian.

(c) p. 128

6.-.23: To the followers of Muhammad, the "people of the Book" were the

(a) true Muslims.
(b) Jews and Christians.
(c) pagans.
(d) Shi'ites.

(b) p. 129

6.-.24: Which of the following is NOT one of the demands made of the followers of the Islamic faith?

(a) prayer toward Mecca five times a day
(b) fasting during the holy month of Ramadan
(c) participation in the jihad or holy war
(d) a pilgrimage to Mecca at least once in one's lifetime

(c) p. 131

6.-.25: The sacred book of Islam is the

(a) Kaaba.
(b) Hegira.
(c) Koran.
(d) Themes.

(c) p. 129

6.-.26: The Dome of the Rock in Jerusalem is holy to Muslims because they believe

(a) Muhammad was born there.
(b) Muhammad died there.
(c) one must visit it for the haji.
(d) Muhammad ascended to heaven from there.

(d) p. 131

6.-.27: Christianity, Islam, and Judaism have several similarities, which include

(a) a belief in monotheism.
(b) belief in the Last Judgement.
(c) the practice of monasticism.
(d) an organized church.

(a) p. 129

6.-.28: The year 1 on the Muslim calendar was marked by

(a) Muhammad's death.
(b) the Arab capture of Medina.
(c) the Prophet's flight from Mecca.
(d) none of the above.

(c) p. 129

6.-.29: In A.D. 711, the Islamic leader Tariq began the rapid conquest of

(a) central Asia.
(b) Spain.
(c) France.
(d) India.

(b) p. 131

6.-.30: The Shi'ite sect of Islam had its origin in

(a) a conflict over the succession to the caliphate.
(b) the question of the divinity of the Prophet.
(c) Muhammad's views on polygamy.
(d) the rejection of the Koran by the Sunnites.

(a) p. 131

6.-.31: Overthrown by the Abbasids, the Umayyad dynasty was able to establish itself in

(a) Egypt.
(b) Spain.
(c) northern India.
(d) Iran.

(b) p. 132

6.-.32: Avicenna's work demonstrated the advanced nature of Muslim

(a) astronomy.
(b) medical knowledge.
(c) maritime exploration.
(d) poetry.

(b) p. 132

6.-.33: The Muslim philosopher whose commentaries on Aristotle were translated into Latin was

(a) Ibn Khaldun.
(b) al-Ma'arri.
(c) Averroes.
(d) Abd ar-Rahman.

(c) p. 133

6.-.34: After Constantine, Byzantium called itself New Rome. (True) p. 115

6.-35: The Byzantine Empire's navy was consistently inferior to the Muslim fleets. (False) p. 118

6.-.36: The Byzantine military possessed a form of flame-throwing weapon. (True) pp. 118, 119

6.-.37: In the context of Byzantine society, childbearing was women's primary social and economic function within the family. (True) p. 120

6.-.38: The conversion of Vladimir had little effect on the Slavic clergy. (False) p. 125

6.-.39: Russian culture was greatly influenced by extensive contacts with western Europe. (False) pp. 125, 126

6.-.40: Russia's conversion to Christianity benefitted its intellectual and literary progress. (False) pp. 125, 126

6.-.41: Byzantine artistic culture had influence long after its political influence declined. (True) p. 127, 128

6.-.42: For Muslim society, the Koran supplied the basis for both religious faith and civil law. (True) p. 129

6.-.43: The stories included in The Arabian Nights are solely of Arabian origin. (False) pp. 133, 134

6.-.44: Consider how it was possible for the "Eastern Rome," Byzantium, to live on for a thousand years after the fall of Rome in the West. Be sure to consider political leadership, economic wealth and power, and military technology in your answer.

6.-.45: The Byzantine Empire successively lost control of areas in the Mediterranean, but gained cultural leadership (if not actual political domination) in the Slavic area of Eastern Europe. Write an essay suggesting why Byzantium was retreating on one front, but advancing on another.

6.-.46: The art and literature of Islam combined the traditions of the past with some spectacular accomplishments of its own. Write an essay showing what modern civilization might have lost, had it not been for the learning and creativity of Islam.

6.-.47: Compare the religious ideas of Muhammad with those of Christians and Jews of the same period, and consider which of his ideas he may have derived from these sources. Consider also the importance of monotheism for Islam, and why Muslims are offended by the use of the term "Mohamadanism."

6.-.48: Part of the history of the relationship between the Christian civilization, both Latin and Greek, and Islam is the history of armed conflict. Consider the battles which took place in the conflict, even before the Crusades, and also the ideology of the jihad, which gave a special religious significance to the wars.

6.-.49: In spite of warfare, peaceful trade and intellectual interchange between Christian and Muslim marked the relationship. Consider several examples of how Islamic civilization either perpetuated important ideas of Greco-Roman civilization, or contributed new ideas of its own to our modern world.

6.-.50: The word "barbarian" was widely used in the Eastern Mediterranean world. Write an essay describing its use in different eras and contexts, giving specific examples.

TEST ITEM FILE

CHAPTER 7: CHURCH AND SOCIETY IN THE MEDIEVAL WEST

7.-.1: Today's historians' understanding of the Middle Ages has been influenced by

(a) new archeological finds and better interpretations of old ones.
(b) new awareness of the richness of Byzantine and Islamic history.
(c) improved understanding of social and women's history.
(d) all of the above.

(d) p. 135

7.-.2: The medieval concept of the three orders of society did NOT include

(a) those who pray.
(b) those who work.
(c) those who trade.
(d) those who fight.

(c) p. 135

7.-.3: In Flanders, industrial expansion centered on

(a) woolen manufacturing.
(b) publishing.
(c) armaments.
(d) ship-building.

(a) p. 136

7.-.4: A charter granted the citizens of a town often included

(a) status as a freeman.
(b) the right to hold a perpetual market.
(c) the right of townsmen to be tried by their own law.
(d) all of the above.

(d) p. 137

7.-.5: The counts of Champagne profited greatly from

(a) the growth of the mining industry in their lands.
(b) selling their subjects' services as mercenaries.
(c) the great fairs that developed in the region.
(d) their close association with the church.

(c) p. 137

7.-.6: Which of the following statements about women in the Middle Ages is NOT true?

(a) Women could inherit land.
(b) Their education was limited to the handicrafts.
(c) Mariolatry and troubadours altered the attitude toward women.
(d) During the later Middle Ages, women greatly outnumbered men.

(b) p. 138

7.-.7: A weapon of the papacy, it may be defined as "regional excommunication."

(a) auctoritas
(b) interdict
(c) investiture
(d) potestas

(b) p. 139

7.-.8: The monastery of Cluny, founded in 910, was significant as the

(a) first Franciscan monastic establishment.
(b) center of a reforming movement that greatly influenced the church.
(c) birthplace of the Albigensian heresy.
(d) none of the above.

(b) p. 140

7.-.9: The Saxon dynasty established by Henry I depended heavily upon them for governing the realm.

(a) bishops
(b) kinsmen
(c) counts
(d) townspeople

(a) p. 141

7.-.10: Hildegard of Bingen was

(a) the author of the "Good Wife."
(b) Queen of France.
(c) head of an important medieval convent.
(d) founder of a dynasty of emperors.

(a) p. 138

7.-.11: The Investiture Controversy was essentially a struggle between

(a) the secular and the regular clergy.
(b) the upper and the lower classes.
(c) the German emperors and the papacy.
(d) Islamic and Germanic warriors.

(c) p. 143

7.-.12: The papacy found military support against the German emperors through an alliance with the

(a) French throne.
(b) Normans of southern Italy.
(c) Byzantine Empire.
(d) Muslims.

(b) p. 144

7.-.13: The conflict between Gregory VII and Emperor Henry IV centered on the issue of

(a) lay investiture.
(b) taxation of the clergy.
(c) the Albigensian heresy.
(d) the wealth of the church.

(a) pp. 143, 144

7.-.14: At Canossa in 1077, Henry IV of Germany

(a) sought papal forgiveness.
(b) deposed Pope Gregory VII.
(c) resigned his office.
(d) signed the Concordat of Worms.

(a) p. 143

7.-.15: A compromise between the pope and the German emperor, the Concordat of Worms stated that

(a) the church had complete control over the appointment of bishops.
(b) clerical elections in Germany would be held in secret.
(c) the emperor would invest bishops with their regalia.
(d) the clergy was exempt from taxes.

(c) p. 143

7.-.16: A critic of the church's wealth, he held that it should return to the ideal of "Apostolic poverty."

(a) Gratian
(b) Arnold of Brescia
(c) Hildebrand
(d) Henry the Proud

(b) p. 145

7.-.17: This was a codification of papal decrees, enactments of church councils, and decisions of church fathers.

(a) <u>Summa Theologica</u>

(b) Decretum
(c) Sic et Non
(d) Defensor Pacis

(b) p. 144

7.-.18: Which of the following statements about Frederick Barbarossa is FALSE?

(a) He was forced to grant virtual independence to the Lombard League.
(b) He made significant concessions to the German princes.
(c) He never visited Italy.
(d) He contributed to the union of Norman Sicily and the German Empire.

(c) p. 145

7.-.19: The medieval pope who came closest to making the concept of a papal monarchy a reality was

(a) Gregory VII.
(b) Benedict IX.
(c) Bernard of Clairvaux.
(d) Innocent III.

(d) pp. 145, 146

7.-.20: A long enduring feud that disturbed the German political scene pitted the house of Hohenstaufen against that of the

(a) Welfs.
(b) Angevins.
(c) Capetians.
(d) Ottonians.

(a) p. 144

7.-.21: The most "modern" of medieval monarchs, this cultivated ruler created a centralized government in Italy.

(a) Philip of Swabia
(b) Otto of Brunswick
(c) Frederick II
(d) Henry IV

(c) pp. 146, 147

7.-.22: In the text, "The Good Wife" and "Women of the Gentle Class" present a medieval conception of women as

(a) being dominated by their husbands.
(b) having equal status with men.
(c) having an active economic and political role in society.
(d) being wicked and untrustworthy.

(a) pp. 138, 140

7.-.23: The policy of independent action pursued by the German princes for centuries following the death of Frederick II's heirs is called

(a) localism.
(b) particularism.
(c) provincialism.
(d) regionalism.

(b) p. 147

7.-.24: A monastic movement directed at the restoration of the ideal of austerity, the Cistercians most famed leader was

(a) Peter Damiani.
(b) Bernard of Clairvaux.
(c) Gerbert of Aurillac.
(d) Francis of Assisi.

(b) p. 149

7.-.25: Their goal was to bring a "revivalist" Christianity to the urban masses and win back heretics.

(a) Albigensians
(b) Augustinians
(c) Ghibellines
(d) Dominicans

(d) p. 149

7.-.26: The <u>universitas</u> or university was originally

(a) an association of guilds of students.
(b) the name given to monastic schools.
(c) the corporation of Masters and Doctors of a faculty.
(d) those who possessed a license to teach.

(a) p. 150

7.-.27: The medieval concept that "universals," encompassing a whole category of things is called

(a) pluralism.
(b) syllogism.
(c) realism.
(d) dualism.

(c) p. 150

7.-.28: His philosophical compromise, called <u>conceptualism</u>, aroused the anger of St. Bernard of Clairvaux.

(a) Albertus Magnus
(b) Peter Abelard
(c) Giotto
(d) John of Salisbury

(b) p. 151

7.-.29: "The state, being nothing more than the individuals who make it up, must serve their interests": this would have been argued by the

(a) Realists.
(b) Dominicans.
(c) Nominalists.
(d) Augustinians.

(c) p. 150

7.-.30: One of the greatest "Schoolmen" or exponents of Scholasticism, he sought to reconcile Aristotelian reason with Christian teachings.

(a) Arnold of Brescia
(b) Thomas Aquinas
(c) Otto of Brunswick
(d) Bonaventura

(b) pp. 151, 152

7.-.31: He argued that the only true source of authority in the commonwealth was the universitas civium, the whole body of the citizens.

(a) Gratian
(b) John of Salisbury
(c) Marsiglio of Padua
(d) John of Fidanza

(c) p. 152

7.-32: The Canticle of the Brother Sun was probably written by

(a) St. James de Compostela.
(b) Robert of Blois.
(c) St. Francis of Assisi.
(d) Innocent III.

(c) p. 152

7.-.33: This Franciscan believed that divine illumination could only come through prayer and love of God.

(a) Bonaventura
(b) Aquinas
(c) John of Salisbury

(d) Bernard of Clairvaux

(a) p. 153

7.-.34: Which of the following was NOT a feature found in Gothic churches?

(a) pointed arches and extensive windows
(b) the use of "flying buttresses"
(c) stained glass
(d) heavy solid walls

(d) pp. 153, 154

7.-.35: His painting was representative of a transition from that of the medieval period to that of the Renaissance.

(a) Giotto
(b) Gelasuis
(c) Dante
(d) Anselm

(a) p. 155

7.-.36: Finance capitalism in the Middle Ages was traditionally condemned as usury. (True) p. 137

7.-.37: Women played an increasingly significant role in the medieval vision of Christianity. (True) p. 138

7.-.38: In the Middle Ages the Jewish people were free to practice their religion and were accepted as equal to Christians (False) p. 139

7.-.39: At the battle of Lechfeld in 955 the Emperor Otto I won a victory and ended the Magyar threat to Germany. (True) p. 141

7.-.40: The trivium studied in the universities of the medieval period was roughly the equivalent of modern day "humanities." (True) p. 149, 150

7.-.41: Consider the proposition that the medieval world seems even more remote from us today than the world of ancient Greece and Rome. Do you agree or disagree? Cite specific historical reasons for your answer.

7.-.42: Describe and analyze the revival of trade and towns in the medieval West after the year 1000.

7.-.43: Historians differ on whether or not the status of women improved in the medieval West. What examples can you cite to show the changing status of women?

7.-.44: What was the Investiture Controversy, and why was it so important during the Middle Ages?

7.-.45: Name and describe three different orders of Christian monks in the West. How did they differ from one another?

7.-.46: The textbook argues that in certain respects the church was a state. Consider the functions of the modern secular state which were practiced by the church during this period. How did the state (in the form of the Empire) respond?

7.-.47: Compare the life of a university student in medieval times with that of students today, in terms of what is studied, the goals of study, and the problems of everyday student life.

7.-.48: Medieval intellectual history uses the terms "nominalism," "realism," and "universals." How did Thomas Aquinas and his use of Aristotle contribute to the debate?

7.-.49: One might argue that religion shows a constant struggle between mysticism and rationality. Give examples of each of these approaches to theology in the Middle Ages.

7.-.50: Some say that the Middle Ages was the "age of faith." Write an essay showing the importance of religion for political, social, and cultural life during that period, using specific examples to demonstrate your points.

TEST ITEM FILE

CHAPTER 8: THE BEGINNINGS OF THE SECULAR STATE

8.-.1: Which of the following was NOT an advantage enjoyed by the strong medieval monarchs of France and England?

(a) the sanctity of kingship
(b) an early sense of unity as nation-states
(c) a national church independent of the pope in Rome
(d) military power to deal with challenges to royal authority

(c) p. 161

8.-.2: The most powerful vassals and rivals of the Capetians were

(a) the counts of Flanders.
(b) the Cathari.
(c) the dukes of Normandy.
(d) the counts of Toulouse.

(c) p. 158

8.-.3: The annulment of Eleanor of Aquitaine's marriage to Louis VII and her subsequent marriage to which of the following made him the greatest landholder in France.

(a) Henry II of England
(b) Duke William of Normandy
(c) Frederick Barbarossa
(d) none of the above

(a) p. 158

8.-.4: King Philip of Augustus of France expanded greatly his territorial holdings at the expense of

(a) the German Empire.
(b) John of England.
(c) the papacy.
(d) Pedro of Castille.

(b) p. 158

8.-.5: The Albigensians held that

(a) the Old Testament's Jehovah was the god of evil.
(b) Jesus was not born of a woman, but was wholly good, wholly light.
(c) Satan created man and the earth.
(d) all of the above.

(d) p. 159

8.-.6: Which of the following benefited the most from the crusade directed against the Albigensians?

(a) the papacy
(b) the Angevins
(c) the French throne
(d) Frederick II Hohenstaufen

(c) pp. 159, 160

8.-.7: Serving as the French throne's investigators, they travelled about the realm to check upon the activities of lesser officials.

(a) bailli
(b) senechal
(c) enqueteurs
(d) prevots

(c) p. 160

8.-.8: King Louis IX of France was viewed by his subjects as a

(a) tyrant.
(b) heretic.
(c) usurper.
(d) benevolent monarch.

(d) pp. 160, 161

8.-.9: The Parlement of France served as

(a) a judicial body.
(b) the royal treasury.
(c) the royal household.
(d) a representative body of the French public.

(a) p. 160

8.-.10: The conflict between Philip IV the Fair of France and Pope Boniface VIII centered on the issue of

(a) the French monarch's failure to persecute heretics.
(b) Philip's efforts to tax the clergy of France.
(c) the pope's support of Philip's foe Edward I of England.
(d) the protection offered the Templars in the face of papal attacks.

(b) pp. 161, 162

8.-.11: The papal bull Unam sanctam, issued by Boniface VIII, declared that

(a) Philip the Fair was excommunicated.

(b) all who desired salvation must be subject to the pope.
(c) the Knights of the Temple were adhering to the Albigensian heresy.
(d) the French must abandon their war with England.

(b) p. 162

8.-.12: Following the death of Boniface VIII the papacy

(a) remained vacant for more than ten years.
(b) was claimed by two rival popes.
(c) began its "Babylonian captivity" in Avignon.
(d) was subject to the control of a council.

(c) p. 162

8.-.13: Which of the following men won the English throne by conquest in 1066?

(a) Harold Godwinson
(b) King Henry of France
(c) the King of Norway
(d) Duke William of Normandy

(d) p. 163

8.-.14: The Domesday Book recorded

(a) those who died at the battle of Hastings.
(b) the gifts of Duke William to the church.
(c) all landed property in England.
(d) those who owed military service to King Edward the Confessor.

(c) p. 164

8.-.15: To avoid military service, Henry I of England allowed his nobles to pay a fee known as

(a) scutage.
(b) fealty.
(c) wergeld.
(d) aid.

(a) p. 165

8.-.16: According to medieval English jurisprudence, laws

(a) were made only by the king.
(b) were made by the king, but only with the approval of the Parliament.
(c) could not be made, as they had always existed.
(d) were made by the curia regis.

(c) p. 165

8.-.17: King Henry II of England imposed by his rule in England by

(a) developing his popularity with a Crusade.
(b) decreeing a common law in the Domesday Book.
(c) arranging for Thomas a Becket to become pope.
(d) destroying hundreds of unlicensed castles.

(d) p. 165

8.-.18: The "common law" was so-called because

(a) it had its roots in the older law of the Anglo-Saxon people.
(b) it was imposed uniformly on the country by William the Conqueror.
(c) it was administered uniformly in the realm by the royal courts.
(d) it had its origins with the people, not the throne.

(c) p. 165

8.-.19: The conflict between King Henry II and Thomas a Becket focused on

(a) the use of the vernacular in church services.
(b) the right of appointment for bishops.
(c) the authority to punish clerics charged with crimes.
(d) the use of presentment in jury cases.

(c) pp. 165, 166

8.-.20: The lasting importance of the Magna Carta is found in its underlying principle that

(a) ultimate authority is vested in the hands of the people.
(b) all men are equal.
(c) the king is not above the law and may be forced to observe it.
(d) Parliament is the representative of the people.

(c) pp. 166, 167

8.-.21: The Magna Carta was agreed to by the English barons and

(a) King John of England.
(b) Richard the Lion Hearted.
(c) William the Conqueror.
(d) Thomas a Becket.

(a) pp. 166, 167

8.-.22: The French equivalent of the English parliament was the

(a) <u>curia regis</u>.
(b) <u>gens du roi</u>.
(c) Parlement.
(d) Estates General.

(d) p. 161

8.-.23: The Statute of Mortmain, enacted in the reign of Edward I, was designed to

(a) place restrictions upon the transfer of land to the church.
(b) deny the exemption of clergymen from taxation.
(c) make all freemen in England subject to military service.
(d) give to Parliament the right to refect ministers named by the king.

(a) p. 168

8.-.24: The Court of the Exchequer dealt with disputes that arose over

(a) land tenures.
(b) criminal matters.
(c) royal finances.
(d) ecclesiastical affairs.

(c) p. 169

8.-.25: The names of Robert Grossteste, Adelard of Bath, and Roger Bacon are associated with

(a) the Magna Carta.
(b) medieval science.
(c) the development of canon law.
(d) none of the above.

(b) p. 169

8.-.26: "In a broad meadow below Aix la Chapelle, the barons meet, their battle has begun."

These lines are from the

(a) troubadours.
(b) Canterbury Tales.
(c) Song of Roland.
(d) Renaissance poet, Dante.

(c) p. 170

8.-.27: The Song of Roland tells the story of

(a) the exploits of the knights of King Arthur's court.
(b) medieval student life.
(c) the courage of Charlemagne's warriors.
(d) the amorous adventures of a German knight.

(c) p. 170, 171

8.-.28: The works of Chretien de Troyes dealt with

(a) courtly love.

(b) the merchant class.
(c) the deeds of crusaders.
(d) the knight Parsifal.

(a) p. 171

8.-.29: In this work, the author is given a guided tour through the realms of the afterlife.

(a) Troilus and Criseyde
(b) Chevalier de la Charette
(c) De Amore
(d) The Divine Comedy

(d) p. 171

8.-.30: Geoffrey Chaucer wrote in

(a) medieval Latin.
(b) classical Latin.
(c) Norman English.
(d) Middle English.

(d) p. 172

8.-.31: In the Canterbury Tales the stories contained are told by

(a) troubadours assembled at the court of Eleanor of Aquitaine.
(b) pilgrims journeying to the tomb of Thomas a Becket.
(c) crusaders returning from the Holy Land.
(d) travelers fleeing from the Black Death who meet at an inn.

(b) p. 172

8.-.32: Hugh Capet and his descendants replaced the Carolingian line on the French throne. (True) p. 157

8.-.33: The term "Babylonian Captivity" refers to a period when the popes resided in France. (True) p. 162

8.-.34: A picture of the Norman Conquest is shown in the Bayeux Tapestry (True) p. 164

8.-.35: By the Salisbury Oath, King William "the Conqueror" of England weakened his power in comparison to that held by the French monarchy. (False) p. 165

8.-.36: The Constitutions of Clarendon were designed to weaken the influence of ecclesiastical courts. (True) p. 166

8.-.37: Oxford University supported some important medieval scientific research. (True) p. 169

8.-.38: Dante Aligheri was an important French troubadour. (False) p. 171

8.-.39: Chaucer's *Canterbury Tales* is a religious book, emphasizing the lives of the saints. (False) p. 172

8.-.40: Using examples from the medieval French and English monarchies, discuss what sets a secular state apart from a state in which church and governance are one.

8.-.41: Write an essay showing the development of the French state from the time of the Capetians to the fourteenth century.

8.-.42: "The Norman Conquest was as important for French history as for English history." Write an essay attacking or defending that statement, citing appropriate examples.

8.-.43: Select three English monarchs from between the Norman Conquest and the end of the fourteenth century and compare their policies and effectiveness.

8.-.44: In medieval France and England there was one institution called the parlement and one called the parliament. Write an essay comparing these two institutions, with specific historical examples.

8.-.45: The Magna Carta is generally believed to be a basic document in English (and also American) history. Write an essay comparing two views of that document, one from the standpoint of an English baron in 1215 and one from a constitutional lawyer in 1995.

8.-.46: Medieval society is sometimes referred to as a hierarchy based on the concept of the vassal. Write an essay describing that hierarchy, including the roles of the monarch, the nobility, the church, and the peasants.

8.-.47: The Middle Ages is sometimes called the "age of chivalry." Describe the code of chivalry, both in literature and in practice, using specific examples.

8.-.48: Medieval kings often had to recognize the rights and privileges of their major vassals, because they had neither the authority nor the power to impose absolute rule. Nowhere was this more clear than with the Magna Carta in England. Describe the importance of this document for the development of the British (and the American) constitution.

8.-.49: What were the elements in the growth of the English and French monarchies which allowed them to assert the power of what was later to become the English and French secular and national states?

8.-.50: Compare the struggle between Philip the Fair of France and Pope Innocent III on the one hand with the struggle between the Hohenstaufens of the Empire and the popes during the Investiture controversy on the other. Who won in each case, and what implications did the victory have for the futures of France and Germany?

TEST ITEM FILE

CHAPTER 9: THE LATE MIDDLE AGES IN EASTERN EUROPE

9.-.1: Which of the following events was NOT important in setting the stage for the Western crusades in the Holy Land?

(a) the Byzantine defeat at Manzikert by the Seljuk Turks in 1071
(b) the tradition of warfare against Muslim forces in Spain
(c) Charlemagne's lack of interest in Jerusalem
(d) the schism between the Eastern and Western Christian churches

(c) p. 174

9.-.2: Pope Gregory VII sent an ambassador to this ruler to discuss joint action against the Turks.

(a) the Byzantine Emperor
(b) The King of England
(c) The German Emperor
(d) Duke William of Normandy

(c) p. 175

9.-.3: At the Council of Clermont he preached the First Crusade, instructing believers to "go forth against the Infidels in a battle worthy to be undertaken now and to be finished in victory."

(a) Urban II
(b) St. Bernard of Clairvaux
(c) Innocent III
(d) St. Dominic

(a) p. 175

9.-.4: Peter the Hermit's army of undisciplined common folk, which took part in the First Crusade,

(a) proved very significant in the final victory.
(b) became well-trained knights after training with the Byzantines.
(c) brought great trouble to the Byzantines by their behavior.
(d) were welcomed by the wealthy of Constantinople.

(c) p. 175

9.-.5: The men of the First Crusade established four crusader states: which of the following was NOT one of these?

(a) Antioch
(b) Edessa
(c) Tripoli

(d) Nicaea

(d) pp. 176, 177

9.-.6: Which of the following military orders did most of its fighting against the pagans of the Baltic region?

(a) the Templars
(b) the Hospitalers
(c) the Teutonic Knights
(d) Santiago de Compostela

(c) p. 177

9.-.7: The Second Crusade was called as a consequence of the fall of

(a) Edessa.
(b) Nicaea.
(c) Jerusalem.
(d) Constantinople.

(a) p. 177

9.-.8: The most famed of the leaders of the Seljuk Turks during the period of the Crusades was

(a) Zangi.
(b) Nureddin.
(c) Tamerlane.
(d) Saladin.

(d) pp. 177, 178

9.-.9: Taking part in the Third Crusade, "the Crusade of the Kings," were all but one of the following monarchs: which one was NOT involved?

(a) Frederick Barbarossa
(b) Frederick of Sicily
(c) Philip Augustus
(d) Richard I "the Lionhearted"

(b) pp. 177, 178

9.-.10: The warriors of the Fourth Crusade were diverted to capture the Christian city of Zara by

(a) Raymond of Toulouse
(b) Innocent III
(c) Enrico Dandolo, doge of Venice
(d) John of England

(c) p. 178

9.-.11: Which of the following benefited most from the Fourth Crusade?

(a) Innocent III
(b) the Venetians
(c) the Byzantines
(d) the French monarchy

(b) pp. 178, 179

9.-.12: Following the recapture of Jerusalem by the Seljuk Turks in 1187, the only Crusade that again gained access to the city for Christians was led by

(a) children.
(b) St. Louis of France.
(c) Richard I "the Lionhearted."
(d) Emperor Frederick II.

(d) p. 244

9.-.13: Which of the following was NOT a consequence of the Crusades?

(a) the introduction into the West of new ideas, words and products
(b) economic prosperity for a number of regions of France
(c) enhancement of the Western nobles' power at the monarchies' expense
(d) a probable long-term weakening of Western religious zeal

(c) p. 180

9.-.14: The so-called "Sicilian Vespers" of 1282 brought to an end his dream of an empire.

(a) Charles of Anjou
(b) Theodore Lascaria
(c) Baldwin of Flanders
(d) Frederick Barbarossa

(a) p. 181

9.-.15: The last century in the Byzantine Empire saw the development of a

(a) number of significant technological advances.
(b) strong monastic revival.
(c) permanent reunion of the Eastern and Western Christian churches .
(d) financial cycle of boom and bust.

(b) pp. 181, 182

9.-.16: By 1363 the Ottoman Turks had established their capital at

(a) Antioch.
(b) Constantinople.
(c) Jerusalem.
(d) Adrianople.

(d) p. 182

9.-.17: Ottoman conquests were delayed for half a century by the revival of the Mongol peril in the person of

(a) Tamerlane.
(b) Hakim.
(c) Zangi.
(d) Selim I, the Grim.

(a) p. 182

9.-.18: The great city of Constantinople fell to the Ottoman Turks in

(a) 1392.
(b) 1453.
(c) 1204.
(d) 1492.

(b) p. 183

9.-.19: Under the Ottomans, the Christian and Jewish people were organized into religious communities or

(a) raya.
(b) millets.
(c) janissaries.
(d) ulema.

(b) p. 183

9.-.20: Which of the following was NOT one of the four subdivisions of the Ottoman ruling class?

(a) men of the emperor
(b) sages
(c) men of the sword
(d) men of the sea

(d) p. 183

9.-.21: In the Ottoman state the *janissaries* were

(a) the Islamic clergy.
(b) a special military unit.
(c) monks.
(d) financial officers.

(b) p. 183

9.-.22: *Ulema* and *muftis* in Ottoman society were

(a) the merchant class.
(b) religious leaders.
(c) classes of slaves.
(d) agricultural workers.

(b) pp. 183, 184

9.-.23: In 1529 the Ottoman armies of Suleiman I, the Magnificent, threatened the city of

(a) Granada.
(b) Vienna.
(c) Kiev.
(d) Rome.

(b) p. 184

9.-.24: Through a series of "capitulations" arranged with the Ottoman Empire, this country increased its own wealth and prestige

(a) England
(b) Russia
(c) Spain
(d) France

(d) p. 184

9.-.25: In the seventeenth century the Ottoman Empire enjoyed military successes under a family of viziers,

(a) the Mongols.
(b) the Muftis.
(c) the Koprulu.
(d) the Seljuk.

(c) p. 186

9.-.26: In the fourteenth century most of western Russia was under the nominal control of the

(a) Teutonic Knights.
(b) Grand Duke of Lithuania.
(c) Ottoman Turks.
(d) Austrians.

(b) p. 186

9.-.27: The city-commonwealth of Novgorod, in contrast to other regions of Russia,

(a) developed a powerful merchant class.
(b) adhered to the Roman Catholic Church.
(c) was free of internal class conflict.
(d) was able to resist the advances of Moscow.

(a) p. 186

9.-.28: Which of the following statements about the conquests of the Mongols is NOT true?

(a) The Poles and Germans were defeated by the horde of Batu Khan.
(b) They subjugated the Mamluks of Egypt in 1260.
(c) The Abbasid caliphate was brought to an end in 1258.
(d) They established the Golden Horde.

(b) p. 187

9.-.29: Which of the following was NOT a factor in Moscow's rise to a position of dominance in Russia?

(a) It had an excellent geographical position.
(b) A series of able princes rule there.
(c) It developed basic representative institutions.
(d) It had support from the Russian Church.

(c) p. 188

9.-.30: The concept of service to the state on the part of the nobles of Russia became universal during the reign of

(a) Ivan the Terrible.
(b) Peter the Great.
(c) Ivan III.
(d) Michael Romanov.

(b) p. 188

9.-.31: The *oprichnina*, created by Ivan the Terrible, was used by him to

(a) bring the church under his control.
(b) break the will of the noble class.
(c) drive the Mongols and Tatars from all Russian lands.
(d) establish the power of Moscow in Poland.

(b) p. 189

9.-.32: A leading figure in Russia's recovery from the anarchy of the "Time of Troubles" was

(a) Boris Godunov.
(b) Kuzma Minin.
(c) the "false Dmitri."
(d) Fedor III Romanov.

(b) p. 189

9.-.33: Czar Michael Romanov came to the throne of Russia as a result of

(a) a military coup.
(b) the influence of the church.
(c) the intervention of the Poles.
(d) an election by the zemski sobor.

(d) p. 189

9.-.34: At his most powerful, the Russian czar ruled as

(a) a constitutional monarch.
(b) an autocrat.
(c) a feudal overlord.
(d) a religious mystic.

(b) pp. 188, 189

9.-.35: The major themes for literature and art in the early Russian state came largely from

(a) the nobility.
(b) the church.
(c) Poland and Germany.
(d) the merchant class.

(b) p. 189

9.-.36: Seeking timber, rope, pitch, and other naval supplies, the merchants of this land were the first to penetrate Russia in any numbers.

(a) China
(b) England
(c) Spain
(d) France

(b) p. 190

9.-.37: The Assizes of Jerusalem was an agreement calling for the reunion of the Greek Orthodox Church and the Catholic Church. (False) p. 177

9.-.38: In the long run, the Crusades tended to weaken the religious zeal of the men of western Europe. (True) p. 180

9.-.39: The attitude of the early Ottoman rulers toward Christians and Jews under their rule was one of intolerance. (False) p. 183

9.-.40: The "new, third Rome" was held by its supporters to be Moscow. (True) p. 188

9.-.41: Describe the strengths and weaknesses of the Crusades, from the pious call of the papacy and Peter the Hermit in the First Crusade, to the brutal struggles of the Fourth Crusade, when Christian fought Christian. What do the Crusades suggest to us about the relationship of religion and warfare?

9.-.42: How did the Muslim forces respond to the initial victories of the Crusaders, and what was the impact of that reaction on European societies?

9.-.43: Write an essay describing the decline and fall of the Roman Empire in the West and the Decline and fall of Byzantium, about 1000 years later. What are the similarities and what are the differences? On the basis of these two examples, can one generalize about the causes of imperial decline?

9.-.44: Write an essay describing the advances of the Ottoman Turks and account for their successes, through the first siege of Vienna.

9.-.45: Compare and contrast the Ottoman system of government with that of the Byzantine Empire which it replaced.

9.-.46: It has been said that Muscovy was blessed by a line of able princes. Describe evolution of Muscovy from submission to the Tatars into the czarist state of the late seventeenth century, noting the contributions of several individual rulers.

9.-.47: Describe the relationship between the Russian czar, the Russian nobility, and the serfs who worked the land. What similarities and what differences do you see between the Russian situation and feudalism in Western Europe at the same period?

9.-.48: Analyze the relationships between Russia and western Europe, including the topics of religion, the economy, the political structure, and culture.

9.-.49: Generally speaking, would you say the relationship between Christians and Muslims during the late Middle Ages had a positive effect on historical development or a negative one? Illustrate your argument with specific examples.

9.-.50: Consider the successor states to the Byzantine Empire: the Russian monarchy to the North and the Ottoman Turkish Empire in the Mediterranean region. To what extent did these states destroy what was left of the old "Roman Empire," and to what extent did they absorb and exploit it?

TEST ITEM FILE

CHAPTER 10: THE RISE OF THE NATION

10.-.1: Which of the following is NOT among the events which characterized the turning point from medieval to modern?

(a) the consolidation of royal authority in France, England, and Spain
(b) the discovery of America
(c) the education of the masses in tax-supported schools
(d) the Renaissance and Reformation

(c) p. 194

10.-.2: At the end of the fifteenth century, "new" monarchs, characterized by the professionalism of their rule, included all of the following EXCEPT

(a) Henry VII.
(b) Louis XI.
(c) Ivan III.
(d) Ferdinand and Isabella.

(c) p. 195

10.-.3: At the opening of the sixteenth century, power in many states of Europe was passing into the hands of the

(a) church.
(b) monarchs.
(c) representative assemblies.
(d) aristocracy.

(b) p. 195

10.-.4: As a consequence of the Black Death which swept Europe in the 1300's,

(a) peasants and workers sought greater rights.
(b) middle class women benefitted.
(c) there was a modest increase in medical knowledge.
(d) all of the above.

(a) pp. 196, 197

10.-.5: The Hundred Years' War was begun by

(a) Philip of Valois.
(b) Edward III of England.
(c) Philip the Fair.
(d) the Black Prince.

(b) p. 198

10.-.6: Which of the following was NOT a cause of the Hundred Years' War?

(a) the English monarch's claim to the French throne
(b) England's continued possession of Aquitaine
(c) English economic interests in Flanders
(d) fears of Turks in the Byzantine empire

(d) pp. 198, 199

10.-.7: The English in the early days of the Hundred Years' War had as a Flemish ally

(a) the Armagnacs.
(b) Philippe de Commynes.
(c) Jacob van Artevelde.
(d) the wealthy oligarchy.

(c) p. 199

10.-.8: At the battle Crecy, the English demonstrated the military merit of

(a) heavy armored cavalry.
(b) the crossbow.
(c) the longbow.
(d) artillery.

(c) p. 199

10.-.9: The goal of Etienne Marcel was to give more voice in French affairs to the

(a) nobility.
(b) Estates General.
(c) king.
(d) church.

(b) p. 199

10.-.10: The movement known as the Jacquerie was

(a) linked to Gallicanism.
(b) a violent peasant uprising.
(c) started by Flemish merchants.
(d) headed by Joan of Arc.

(b) p. 199

10.-.11: The assassination of Louis, duke of Orleans, led to a bitter feud between the Armagnacs and the

(a) Burgundians.
(b) Orleanists.
(c) followers of Etienne Marcel.

(d) great nobles of France.

(a) p. 200

10.-.12: Joan of Arc, the peasant girl from Lorraine, stood as a symbol of

(a) the Jacquerie.
(b) French anti-royalism.
(c) French patriotism.
(d) anti-papal feelings.

(c) pp. 200, 201

10.-.13: Bastard feudalism refers to the fact that

(a) the European nobles had many illegitimate children.
(b) the papacy brought moral pressure on monarchs to reform.
(c) service in the late medieval armies was based on money more than feudal loyalty.
(d) all of the above.

(c) p. 194

10.-.14: The *taille*, granted the French monarch in 1439, was a

(a) victory over the church.
(b) triumph for the peasants.
(c) direct tax.
(d) new political office.

(c) p. 200

10.-.15: The policy known as Gallicanism represented a limitation in France of the power of the

(a) king.
(b) Estates General.
(c) papacy.
(d) English.

(c) p. 201

10.-.16: The Pragmatic Sanction of Bourges confirmed the

(a) sainthood of Joan of Arc.
(b) French annexation of Flanders.
(c) policy of Gallicanism.
(d) abolition of the Estates General.

(c) p. 201

10.-.17: At Bannockburn in 1314, Edward II of England suffered a military defeat at the hands of the

(a) forces of Joan of Arc.
(b) Scots.
(c) Irish allies of France.
(d) armies of Flanders.

(b) p. 203

10.-.18: The Vision Concerning Piers Plowman represented a defense of

(a) the interest of the impoverished English landowners.
(b) the English clergy against the attacks of the Lollard.s
(c) the peasantry of England.
(d) King Edward III.

(c) p. 203

10.-.19: The Statutes of Provisors and Praemunire were designed to limit in England the power of the

(a) nobles.
(b) papacy.
(c) parliament.
(d) merchant class.

(b) p. 203

10.-.20: Which of the following was NOT involved in the movement led by John Wycliffe?

(a) nationalism.
(b) anti-papal feelings.
(c) social and economic unrest.
(d) anti-war feelings.

(d) pp. 204, 205

10.-.21: As Parliament divided into two houses, the "House of Commons" was composed of

(a) the lower clergy.
(b) peasants.
(c) knights and burgesses.
(d) earls and barons.

(c) p. 204

10.-.22: John Ball and Wat Tyler were leading figures in the

(a) "Model Parliament."
(b) War of the Roses.
(c) Peasants' Revolt of 1381.
(d) Lancaster-York struggle.

(c) p. 204

10.-.23: The figure of Robin Hood is first referred to in

(a) Piers Plowman.
(b) The Prince.
(c) the works of John Wycliffe.
(d) the revolt of Owen Glendower.

(a) p. 205

10.-.24: The first English monarch of the house of Lancaster was

(a) Richard II.
(b) Henry VII.
(c) Henry IV.
(d) Edward III.

(c) p. 205

10.-.25: Richard III, the last Yorkist king of England, has been blamed for the

(a) final defeat of England in the Hundred Years' War.
(b) murder of the "Little Princes", Edward V and his brother.
(c) defeat of the Peasants' Revolt.
(d) untimely death of Henry V.

(b) p. 205

10.-.26: The first Tudor monarch, Henry VII, came to the throne of England following his victory

(a) on Bosworth Field.
(b) at Agincourt.
(c) in the War of the Roses.
(d) over John Ball and Wat Tyler.

(a) p. 206

10.-.27: Henry VII Tudor set the stage for his successors by all of the following EXCEPT

(a) pursuing new fiscal policies.
(b) arguing with the pope over control of the church.
(c) restoring the prestige of the English monarchy.
(d) fixing the pattern of crown relations with Parliament.

(b) p. 206

10.-.28: In addition to Columbus' voyage, the year 1492 was a critical year for Spain because it saw

(a) Aragon and Castile united.

(b) the issuance of the Golden Bull.
(c) the reconquest of Muslim Granada.
(d) the end of the Great Schism.

(c) p. 208

10.-.29: Ferdinand and Isabella enhanced royal control over Spain by all of the following ways EXCEPT

(a) creating the Council of Castile..
(b) bringing the church under royal discipline.
(c) accepting the Jews fully into Spanish society.
(d) introducing the Spanish Inquisition.

(c) p. 208

10.-.30: The Spanish Inquisition was used by Ferdinand and Isabella to do all of the following EXCEPT

(a) promote Spanish nationalism.
(b) force Christianity on Spanish Jews.
(c) enforce universal Catholicism.
(d) destroy Lutheranism.

(d) p. 208

10.-.31: The chief targets of the Inquisition included which of the following?

(a) Muslims.
(b) Jews.
(c) Marranos.
(d) all of the above.

(d) p. 208

10.-.32: Following the Great Interregnum, the first German emperor was

(a) Charles V.
(b) Charles the Bold.
(c) Rudolf of Habsburg.
(d) Conrad IV.

(c) p. 208

10.-.33: The purpose of the Golden Bull of 1356 was to

(a) determine the method by which the German emperor was selected.
(b) limit papal authority in the Swiss Confederation.
(c) forbid the Inquisition in many of the German states.
(d) confirm the union of Austria and Burgundy.

(a) p. 208

10.-.34: The Hansa was the name given to

(a) the German electors.
(b) the Swiss forest cantons.
(c) German mercenaries.
(d) an organization of merchant cities.

(d) p. 208

10.-.35: The Englishman Sir John Hawkwood was an early example of a

(a) maritime explorer.
(b) Conciliarist.
(c) <u>condottiere</u>.
(d) <u>ministeriales</u>.

(c) p. 209

10.-.36: The term "Great Schism" refers to

(a) the Civil war in France between Burgundians and Armagnacs.
(b) a period when two popes each claimed to rule the church.
(c) the conflict between the Guelfs and Ghibellines.
(d) the religious revolt of Jan Hus.

(b) p. 210

10.-.37: The Guelf-Ghibelline conflict long disturbed the political stability of

(a) England.
(b) Italy.
(c) France.
(d) Spain.

(b) p. 209

10.-.38: The "Great Schism" came to an end with the

(a) Council of Constance.
(b) Pragmatic Sanction of Bourges.
(c) enactment of the Golden Bull.
(d) Council of Basel.

(a) p. 210

10.-.39: The uprising of the *ciompi* in 1378 was an example of mounting

(a) peasant violence.
(b) religious unrest.
(c) urban social conflict.
(d) <u>condottieri</u> despotism.

(c) p. 212

10.-.40: The Golden Book was a

(a) vernacular translation of the Bible used by Jan Hus.
(b) guidebook to heresies used by the Inquisition.
(c) listing of the old merchant families of Venice.
(d) first instruction manual for artillery men.

(c) p. 213

10.-.41: The political lessons learned in the "school of Europe" were first set down in

(a) The Prince.
(b) Piers Plowman.
(c) the Golden Bull.
(d) de Commynes' Memoirs.

(a) p. 213

10.-.42: Europe in the late 1300s suffered from a severe shortage of labor. (True) p. 195

10.-.43: England in the 1300s had significant economic ties with the Flemish region. (True) pp. 198, 199

10.-.44 After 1483 the Holy Roman emperors, though still elected, were from the house of Burgundy. (False) p. 215

10.-.45: The career of Jacquer Coeur was an example of a military man who achieved political power through force. (False) pp. 201, 202

10.-.46: The authors refer to the late Middle Ages as a "world turned upside down." Write an essay describing this upside down world, addressing the decline of health and wealth and also changes in the social structure which undermined the power of medieval elites.

10.-.47: Consider the importance of dynastic ties during the growth of national monarchies in the late Middle Ages. What was the importance of the family ties to the struggle between France and England, to the fight for the English crown, and to the link between Spain and the Holy Roman empire?

10.-.48: Compare and contrast the parts of Europe which are developing toward national monarchies and those which are maintaining their decentralized medieval characteristics during the late Middle Ages. Be sure to give examples of the importance of elective versus hereditary monarchy, the role of the church, and physical geography in your considerations.

10.-.49: Early in the 1400's Christians, Muslims, and Jews all played important roles in the Iberian peninsula. By 1500, however, that situation had changed dramatically. Describe the change and how it came about.

10.-.50: Machiavellian statecraft came as a shock to many people who believed in the ideal of a Christian monarchy. Describe the realities of the political life of the late Middle Ages which set the stage for Machiavelli's *Prince*.

TEST ITEM FILE

CHAPTER 11: THE RENAISSANCE

11.-.1: Scholars of the first half of the nineteenth century would have argued that the Renaissance was the

(a) intellectual awakening that came with the Reformation.
(b) rebirth of the classical values of Greece and Rome.
(c) intellectual reawakening of the Carolingian period.
(d) twelfth century economic upturn.

(b) p. 216

11.-.2: Trade in the 1300s declined markedly as a result of

(a) numerous wet summers.
(b) the Black Death.
(c) the Hundred Years' War.
(d) all of the above.

(d) p. 217

11.-.3: Which of the following is NOT a correct statement about the Renaissance?

(a) During the Renaissance the economy of western Europe changed from one based on barter to one based on money.
(b) Women gained significant prestige and individual rights.
(c) The uncovering of classical works both helped and hindered scientific development.
(d) Leading artists such as Dürer, Michelangelo, and da Vinci brought the visual arts to a new height.

(b) p. 234

11.-.4: Venetian trader by the 1300s went from London in the West as far East as

(a) Alexandria in Egypt.
(b) Constantinople.
(c) the Crimean region of Russia.
(d) China.

(d) p. 218

11.-.5: In the 1300s, the largest industrial establishment in Europe was probably the Venetian arsenal, which was devoted to

(a) woolen manufacturing.
(b) mining.
(c) printing of books.
(d) ship building.

(d) p. 219

11.-.6: During the Renaissance, European manufacturing was achieved by subcontracting work in the

(a) put-out system.
(b) arsenals.
(c) ciompi.
(d) galleys.

(a) p. 219

11.-.7: Which of the following was NOT involved in Renaissance banking?

(a) Cosimo de' Medici
(b) the Fugger family
(c) Jacques Coeur
(d) Marsilio Ficino

(d) p. 219

11.-.8: The enclosure, or fencing off, of common pasture lands in England in the sixteenth century, was designed to foster the interests of

(a) the mining industry.
(b) sheep-raisers.
(c) capitalist agriculturists.
(d) grape-growers.

(b) p. 219

11.-.9: By 1500 the leading patrons of intellectual and artistic pursuits in Italy were

(a) monks.
(b) the feudal nobility.
(c) the *ciompi*.
(d) the wealthy bourgeoisie.

(d) p. 220

11.-.10: The Platonic Academy, the intellectual center of Florence, was subsidized by

(a) Lorenzo "the Magnificent" de' Medici.
(b) Pope Sixtus VI.
(c) Giovanni Palestrina.
(d) Manuel Chrysoloras.

(a) p. 220

11.-.11: The most important invention of the Renaissance was the

(a) compass.
(b) astrolabe.

(c) printing press.
(d) chronometer.

(c) p. 220

11.-.12: A significant center for the spreading of old tales and new ideas was the *veillee* or

(a) church service.
(b) village gathering.
(c) guild hall.
(d) urban rallies.

(b) p. 220

11.-.13 The Tuscan dialect, a vernacular tongue, only received recognition as a literary language with the appearance of

(a) Petrarch's Scipio Africanus.
(b) Dante's Divine Comedy.
(c) Machiavelli's The Prince.
(d) Vergil's Aeneid.

(b) p. 221

11.-.14: The Song of Roland was written in

(a) medieval Latin.
(b) langue d'oil.
(c) Provencal.
(d) Tuscan.

(b) p. 220

11.-.15: Through their studies, the humanists came to hold in highest esteem the values of

(a) the medieval church.
(b) classical antiquity.
(c) the scientists.
(d) the Protestant Reformation.

(b) p. 221

11.-.16: The first major writer to embody a number of the characteristics of the Renaissance was

(a) Petrarch.
(b) Dante Alighieri.
(c) Vesalius.
(d) Giovanni Boccaccio.

(b) p. 221

11.-.17: A group of Florentines, gathered in a country villa to escape the Black Death, tell earthy and entertaining tales in Boccaccio's

(a) Decameron.
(b) Colloquies.
(c) In Praise of Folly.
(d) Canterbury Tales.

(a) p. 221

11.-.18: The humanists of the Platonic Academy focused their attention upon

(a) Greek studies.
(b) scientific inquiry.
(c) mathematics.
(d) technological advance.

(a) p. 222

11.-.19: His fame rests upon his demonstration that the so-called Donation of Constantine was a forgery.

(a) Pico della Mirandola
(b) Lorenzo Valla
(c) Erasmus
(d) Cosimo de' Medici

(b) p. 222

11.-.20: His works included both biblical scholarship and mocking satire.

(a) Valla
(b) Aldus Manutius
(c) Harvey
(d) Erasmus

(d) p. 223

11.-.21: "In all their rule, and strictest tie of their order there was but this one clause to be observed, Do What Thou Will." This passage described Gargantua and Pantagruel, who were the literary creations of

(a) Galen.
(b) Josquin des Pres.
(c) Caravaggio.
(d) Rabelais.

(d) p. 223

11.-.22: In the Renaissance, "Carnival" represented for the peasantry a period of

(a) religious meditation.

(b) open lust and aggression.
(c) pious fasting.
(d) homage to their lords.

(b) p. 224

11.-.23: In the Renaissance the advance of science was impeded by

(a) the humanists' increasing access to ancient scientific authorities.
(b) the Scholastic tradition.
(c) the humanists' view that ancient authorities were above criticism.
(d) all of the above.

(c) p. 224

11.-.24: Which of the following was an advance in technology initially made by the Chinese?

(a) paper manufacturing.
(b) gunpowder.
(c) movable type.
(d) all of the above.

(d) p. 224

11.-.25: Gunpowder was first used in Europe during the

(a) Fifth Crusade.
(b) Hundred Years' War.
(c) War of the Roses.
(d) the siege of Constantinople.

(b) p. 225

11.-.26: Which of the following persons did NOT make significant advances in the study of medicine during the Renaissance?

(a) Ambrose Pare
(b) Andreas Vesalius
(c) Paracelsus
(d) Nicolaus Copernicus

(d) pp. 225, 226

11.-.27: The geocentric theory of antiquity was attacked in the sixteenth century by

(a) Isaac Newton.
(b) Nicolaus Copernicus.
(c) Ptolemy.
(d) Leonardo da Vinci.

(b) p. 226

11.-.28: Which of the following developments in the field of music occurred during the Renaissance?

(a) the invention of the organ
(b) the emergence of paid professional musicians
(c) music became part of the popular culture
(d) all of the above

(d) p. 226

11.-.29: Which of the following statements regarding the Renaissance is true?

(a) It made the Reformation inevitable.
(b) Humanism was directed exclusively against Christianity.
(c) Popes of the period were deeply involved in the arts and learning.
(d) The average intellectual level of the clergy advanced markedly.

(c) p. 227

11.-.30: In art, *chiaroscuro* refers to

(a) the use of perspective in painting.
(b) the use of oil paints.
(c) a technique stressing contrasts of light and shade.
(d) pigments applied to wet plaster on a wall.

(c) p. 227

11.-.31: Brueghel and Bosch were leading Renaissance artists from

(a) France.
(b) Germany.
(c) Italy.
(d) the Low Countries.

(d) p. 229

11.-.32: The artistic center of the Renaissance in Italy was

(a) Florence.
(b) Rome.
(c) Milan.
(d) Venice.

(a) p. 227

11.-.33: Desiring to decorate the walls and ceilings of the Sistine Chapel, the pope employed

(a) Titian.
(b) Leonardo da Vinci.
(c) Michelangelo Buonarotti.
(d) Botticelli.

(c) p. 229

11.-.34: His paintings of "The Knight, Death, and the Devil" and other grim figures of the Apocalypse reflected the Gothic strain seen in northern art.

(a) Albrecht Durer
(b) Jacob Fugger
(c) Benvenuto Cellini
(d) Johann Reuchlin

(c) p. 321

11.-.35: The first sculptor of the Renaissance was

(a) Andrea Palladio.
(b) Donatello.
(c) Benvenuto Cellini.
(d) Castiglione.

(b) p. 230

11.-.36: The colossal statue of David as well as the Pieta were the creations of

(a) Leonardo da Vinci.
(b) Giorgio Maggiore.
(c) Michelangelo Buonarotti
(d) Albrecht Durer.

(c) p. 232

11.-.37: Which of the following statements about society and life in the era of the Renaissance is NOT true?

(a) The peasantry probably lived better after the Black Death than before it.
(b) The upper classes of Italy began to eat with forks, not their fingers.
(c) Improvement of roads and greater security made travel easier.
(d) Women were prime consumers of printed books.

(d) pp. 232-235.

11.-.38: The Courtier, a book on Renaissance manners, was written by

(a) Francesco Guicciardini.
(b) Christine de Pisan.
(c) Baldassare Castiglione.
(d) Lorenzo Valla.

(c) p. 234

11.-.39: During the Renaissance, the economy of western Europe changed from one based on money to one based on barter. (False) p. 235

11.-.40: Galleys, caravels, and fluyts can be considered the first European tools of conquest. (True) p. 218

11.-.41: The major bankers of Europe in the late Middle Ages were Italians. (True) p. 219

11.-.42: Petrarch's fame as a Renaissance writer in part rests on his vernacular love sonnets. (True) p. 221

11.-.43: Lorenzo Valla revealed the forgery of the "Donation of Constantine." (True) p. 235

11.-.44: Women in the Renaissance period enjoyed a status much greater than that seen in the medieval period. (False) p. 235

11.-.45: Describe the meaning of the word "renaissance," both in its literal meaning and in historical use. Why can one speak of several "renaissances" in addition to THE RENAISSANCE which began in Italy in the fourteenth century?

11.-.46: Write an essay responding critically to the following statement: "The Renaissance was a period of artistic renewal but also a period of economic stagnation."

11.-.47: Describe and analyze the roles of the Medici family of Florence during the Renaissance, noting their political, social, and artistic influences.

11.-.48: The Church played various roles in Renaissance life, ranging from the arts to politics. Write an essay analyzing the role of the Church, taking note of the contributions of both Michelangelo and Erasmus.

11.-.49: Much emphasis is placed upon the ideal of the "Renaissance man" as courtier, gentleman, and humanist. Write an essay comparing the life of the elitist Renaissance man with the lives of people not so favored, women and blacks.

11.-.50: Popular culture during the Renaissance flowered as well as did the "fine arts." Write an essay on everyday life in the Renaissance, noting the importance of "carnival" and religion.

TEST ITEM FILE

CHAPTER 12: THE PROTESTANT REFORMATION

12.-.1: More than a spiritual upheaval, the Protestant Reformation represented a significant

(a) intellectual upheaval.
(b) economic revolution.
(c) social revolution.
(d) all of the above.

(d) p. 237

12.-.2: Martin Luther, in his teachings, emphasized

(a) good works.
(b) the role of the clergy.
(c) justification by faith.
(d) ritual.

(c) p. 239

12.-.3: Which of the following was an important Christian reform movement prior to Luther's Reformation?

(a) the Anabaptists.
(b) the Henry VIII's conflict with the papacy.
(c) the idealism of Nicholas Copernicus.
(d) the Brethren of the Common Life.

(d) p. 238

12.-.4: The popular work Imitation of Christ was written by

(a) Thomas a Kempis.
(b) Erasmus.
(c) Lucas Cranach.
(d) Thomas Muntzer.

(a) p. 238

12.-.5: Briefly the virtual dictator of Florence, calling for the destruction of the "vanities" of society, he died at the stake.

(a) Sebastian Castellio
(b) Domenico Scandella
(c) Girolamo Savonarola
(d) John Eck

(c) p. 238

12.-.6: At the time of his break with the church of Rome, Martin Luther was a

(a) Jesuit.
(b) law student.
(c) Augustinian monk.
(d) merchant.

(c) p. 238

12.-.7: The specific incident that led Luther to post his Ninety-Five Theses was

(a) the "sale" of indulgences.
(b) Ulrich Zwingli's execution.
(c) the Council of Constance.
(d) a frightening thunderstorm.

(a) p. 238

12.-.8: The papacy found itself in need of money in 1517 to pay for

(a) a new Crusade.
(b) the rebuilding of St. Peter's.
(c) its war with the Calvinists.
(d) defense against the Ottomans.

(b) p. 238

12.-.9: By drawing upon the "Treasury of Merit" the papacy held that it could grant individuals

(a) forgiveness of sins.
(b) salvation.
(c) a remission of penance.
(d) all of the above.

(c) p. 238

12.-.10: Luther's affirmation of the concept of "every man his own priest" represented a denial of the need of the

(a) Bible.

(b) the priesthood.
(c) act of "good works."
(d) sacraments.

(b) p. 239

12.-.11: Threatened with arrest by the Catholic authorities, Luther was protected by

(a) Charles V Habsburg.
(b) Frederick the Wise of Saxony.
(c) the Hussites.
(d) John Eck.

(b) p. 239

12.-.12: Which of the following was NOT a factor in the success of Luther's religious movement?

(a) the printing press
(b) German nationalism
(c) the German emperor's support
(d) the support of German princes

(c) p. 240

12.-.13: Charles V Habsburg's response to the Reformation was influenced by his

(a) fundamental opposition to the papacy.
(b) preoccupation with the many political problems confronting him.
(c) conflict with the ruling dynasty of Spain.
(d) deep sense of his own sinfulness.

(b) p. 241

12.-.14: The League of Schmalkalden was the

(a) alliance of Calvinist, Anabaptist, and Lutheran theologians.
(b) military arm of the Protestant princes and cities.
(c) French-Spanish anti-Protestant alliance.
(d) union of Swiss cantons under Calvin.

(b) p. 240

12.-.15: The Peace of Augsburg of 1555 established the principle that

(a) religious freedom would be established throughout the empire.

(b) complete separation of church and state would be recognized.
(c) the religion of each state would be determined by its prince.
(d) religious toleration existed in all the German states.

(c) p. 241

12.-.16: In 1525 the Teutonic Knights

(a) were disbanded and their lands became the Lutheran duchy of Prussia.
(b) threw their support to Charles V Habsburg.
(c) were defeated by the Greek Orthodox forces of Moscow.
(d) subdued the Swedes and converted them to Lutheranism.

(a) p. 241

12.-.17: An important element of support for the Reformation was found in

(a) the urban areas.
(b) the monastic establishments.
(c) northern Italy.
(d) the serf class.

(a) p. 241

12.-.18: The Peasants' Revolt of 1524-1525 was directed against the

(a) mendicant orders of the church.
(b) manorial lords.
(c) wandering merchants.
(d) preachers of popular religion.

(b) p. 242

12.-.19: "The princes of the world are gods, the common people are Satan," was a view expressed by

(a) Pope Alexander VI.
(b) Martin Luther.
(c) John Calvin.
(d) John Knox.

(b) p. 242

12.-.20: The Reformation in Switzerland was begun by

(a) Thomas Cranmer.
(b) William Tyndale.
(c) Ulrich Zwingli.

(d) Michael Servetus.

(c) p. 242

12.-.21: The Reformation movement as initiated in Switzerland denied

(a) Christ's divinity.
(b) the right of the clergy to marry.
(c) the miraculous nature of the sacrament of the Eucharist.
(d) moral role of Christianity in people's everyday lives.

(c) p. 243

12.-.22: The doctrine of "consubstantiation" was held by

(a) Martin Luther.
(b) the Catholic Church.
(c) John Calvin.
(d) the Church of England.

(a) pp. 243, 244

12.-.23: The Institutes of the Christian Religion was written by

(a) John Eck.
(b) John of Leiden.
(c) John Calvin.
(d) Thomas Erastus.

(c) p. 243

12.-.24: John Calvin's "City of God," a Protestant Rome, was established in

(a) Geneva.
(b) Lyon.
(c) Munich.
(d) Dresden.

(a) p. 243

12.-.25 Which of the following regions did NOT fall under the influence of Calvinism?

(a) Scotland
(b) the Low Countries
(c) New England
(d) Austria

(d) p. 243

12.-.26: In France, the followers of John Calvin were called

(a) Huguenots.
(b) Anabaptists.
(c) Mennonites.
(d) Puritans.

(a) p. 244

12.-.27: A primary factor in Henry VIII's break with the Catholic Church was

(a) his hatred of Charles V.
(b) the influence of the Lollards.
(c) England's conflict with Spain.
(d) his desire for a legitimate male heir.

(d) p. 244

12.-.28: The Act of Supremacy of 1534

(a) declared the pope superior to all church councils.
(b) named the king the supreme head of the English Church.
(c) set forth the Protestant doctrine of the Trinity.
(d) proclaimed the Switzerland of John Calvin a theocracy.

(b) p. 244

12.-.29: Particularly hard hit by the establishment of the Anglican Church in England were the

(a) noble landlords.
(b) free peasants.
(c) monastic establishments.
(d) merchant classes.

(c) p. 244

12.-.30: An example of the "left wing" of the Reformation movement was to be seen in the

(a) Anabaptists.
(b) Anglican High Church.
(c) the Calvinists of Geneva.
(d) Capuchin order.

(a) p. 245

12.-.31: Rejecting the Trinity in the hope of reconciling Judaism, Islam, and Christianity, this Unitarian was burned at the stake by Calvin.

(a) Michael Servetus
(b) Thomas Cranmer
(c) Sebastian Castellio
(d) Savonarola

(a) p. 245

12.-.32: Which of the following was NOT one of the "common denominators" of the Protestant sects?

(a) repudiation of Rome's claim as the one true faith
(b) an appeal to primitive Christianity
(c) a tolerant attitude toward other Protestant groups
(d) a reduction in the number of sacraments

(c) p. 245

12.-.33: In terms of "radicalness," which of the following would be considered the most distant theologically from the Catholic Church?

(a) the Church of England
(b) the Calvinists
(c) the Lutherans
(d) the Anabaptists

(d) p. 245

12.-.34: The Thirty-Nine Articles may be said to have been the constitution of

(a) John of Leiden's movement.
(b) the Mennonites.
(c) Swiss Calvinism.
(d) the Church of England.

(d) p. 246

12.-.35: According to this reformer, salvation was only for the predestined elect, and only achieved through God's grace.

(a) Jacobus Arminius
(b) John Calvin
(c) Martin Luther
(d) Thomas Erastus

(b) p. 246

12.-.36: Though not wholly opposed to sexual intercourse, they believed that it should be limited to married couples.

(a) Calvinists
(b) Lutherans
(c) Catholics
(d) all of the above

(d) p. 247

12.-.37: Arminianism tends to adhere to the doctrine of

(a) free will.
(b) theocracy.
(c) predestination.
(d) consubstantiation.

(a) p. 247

12.-.38: Erastianism argued that

(a) heretics should be legally free.
(b) church and state should be separate.
(c) the state should rule the church.
(d) the church should rule the state.

(d) p. 246

12.-.39: A new Catholic order, founded during the Reformation, it took a lead in the education of young women.

(a) Oratory of Divine Love
(b) Capuchins
(c) Ursulines
(d) Mennonites

(c) p. 248

12.-.40: Which of the following regions contained virtually no Protestants by the year 1600?

(a) Poland
(b) France
(c) Spain
(d) all of the above

(b) p. 251 (map)

12.-.41: In the areas of social, economic, and political activity Luther's views were more liberal than most Protestant reformers. (False) p. 241

12.-.42: John of Leiden and his followers reflected a more radical aspect of the Protestant Reformation. (True) p. 245

12.-.43: The Inquisition was a major force in halting the spread of Protestantism in northern Europe. (False) p. 250

12.-.44: The Protestant and Catholic Reformations had no effect on the role of women in sixteenth-century society. (False) p. 252

12.-.45: Nationalism was a factor in the triumph of Protestantism in some regions. (True) p. 253

12.-.46: Write an essay describing what was "protestant" about the religious reform movements of the sixteenth century. Did the reforms come only from those who called themselves Protestants, or were there Catholic reformers too?

12.-.47: Describe the roles of Martin Luther, John Calvin, and Ignatius Loyola in the reforms of the sixteenth century. To what extent did they react against each other?

12.-.48: What was the role of the controversy over "faith alone," "free will," and "predestination" in the theological controversies of the reformation?

12.-.49: Write an essay analyzing the Protestant groups from a political point of view, noting the importance of the cities and early nationalism, the ambitions of the monarchs, and desire to prevent social and political revolutions.

12.-.50: To what extent did the Protestant Reformation and the Catholic Reformation have modernizing influence on Western Civilization, leading to such movements as capitalism and democracy? Why do some historians today view the debates over the modernity question relatively unproductive?

TEST ITEM FILE

CHAPTER 13: THE GREAT POWERS IN CONFLICT

13.-.1: The textbook suggests that there is no general agreement on what date best divides the medieval from the modern. Which of the following is NOT a good candidate for such a date?

(a) 1485, when both Spain and England experienced political centralization
(b) 1492, when Columbus made his first discoveries
(c) 1500, the fabled millenium-and-a-half of Christian scripture
(d) 1517, the outbreak of Luther's reformation

(c) p. 256

13.-.2: The "long sixteenth century" or *long durée* saw all but one of the following developments: which one did NOT occur?

(a) the Mediterranean remained Europe's economic and military heart
(b) there was a steady growth in population
(c) it was a period of price inflation
(d) European agriculture greatly increased the food supply

(d) p. 257

13.-.3: By the end of the Middle Ages in the West most smaller feudal units had been absorbed into larger states except in

(a) Spain and Portugal.
(b) Scandinavia.
(c) Germany and Italy.
(d) France.

(c) p. 258

13.-.4: Which of the following was NOT one of the dominant states in the early modern period?

(a) England
(b) France
(c) Spain
(d) Italy

(d) p. 258

13.-.5: In the fifteenth and sixteenth centuries it was a major power in the central Danube valley.

(a) Muscovite Russia
(b) the Ottoman Empire

(c) Poland-Lithuania
(d) Hungary

(b) p. 277 (map)

13.-.6: By 1500 most sovereign states of Europe had as an instrument of foreign policy

(a) a professional diplomatic corps.
(b) a professional army.
(c) neither of the above.
(d) both of the above.

(d) pp. 257, 258

13.-.7: Armies of the early modern centuries were normally composed of

(a) the drafted civilians.
(b) citizen soldiers.
(c) mercenaries.
(d) the middle classes.

(c) p. 259

13.-.8: Which of the following statements regarding the "long sixteenth century" is NOT true?

(a) Naval supremacy passed from the Mediterranean to the Atlantic.
(b) Trade between Italy and the Levant was disrupted.
(c) The Dutch moved toward a dominant position in world trade.
(d) Municipal governments' role in state affairs diminished.

(d) p. 259

13.-.9: Which of the following statements regarding Charles VIII of France's invasion of Italy IS true?

(a) The Italy was briefly annexed by the French troops.
(b) It provoked the first great modern coalition, the Holy League.
(c) England, involved in the Reformation crisis, remained neutral.
(d) It hindered the spread of Renaissance thought to other lands.

(b) p. 260

13.-.10: In 1527 the city of Rome fell to

(a) the Ottoman Turks.
(b) French mercenaries.
(c) troops of Charles V Habsburg.
(d) Italian condottieri.

(c) 261

13.-.11: In his long struggle with Charles V Habsburg, Francis I of France was allied with

(a) Protestant England.
(b) the Ottoman emperor.
(c) Greek Orthodox Russia.
(d) the king of Spain.

(b) p. 260

13.-.12: Philip II of Spain also held as his possession all of the following EXCEPT

(a) the Netherlands.
(b) Milan and Naples.
(c) Mexico and Peru.
(d) Austria.

(d) p. 261

13.-.13: Which of the following was NOT one of the problems confronting Philip II of Spain?

(a) the revolt of the Dutch Protestants
(b) the threat of the English and French to Spain's overseas holdings
(c) the spread of the Reformation within Spain
(d) the threat of Ottoman naval power in the Mediterranean

(c) p. 261

13.-.14: In the Netherlands the unifying religious force came from

(a) Lutheranism.
(b) Calvinism.
(c) Unitarianism.
(d) Anabaptism.

(b) pp. 261, 262

13.-.15: Prince William of Orange led the people of this region in their struggle for independence.

(a) Huguenot France.
(b) the Netherlands.
(c) Scotland.
(d) Switzerland.

(b) p. 262

13.-.16: Which of the following was NOT characteristic of the Renaissance monarchs?

(a) the existence of some form of representative assembly
(b) increasing bureaucratic organization
(c) the disappearance of localism within the state

(d) a loss of power by the great nobles

(c) p. 262

13.-.17: All of the following contributed to the cultural flowering of "the Spanish century" EXCEPT

(a) Cervantes.
(b) El Greco.
(c) St. Teresa of Avila.
(d) Leonardo da Vinci.

(d) p. 264

13.-.18: A major contributing factor to the stagnation of the Spanish economy during the early seventeenth century was

(a) the financial difficulty of the papacy.
(b) the economic decline of the Hanseatic League.
(c) Philip II's wars in Europe.
(d) Spain's loss of Central America to the British.

(c) p. 358

13.-.19: The fueros and justicia mayor of Spain were examples of

(a) special privileges enjoyed by different regions of that country.
(b) officers of the crown who carried royal power into the provinces.
(c) royal officials in the New World.
(d) inspectors and powers of the Inquisition.

(c) p. 264

13.-.20: While Spain gained immense wealth from its colonies, its economy was greatly weakened by

(a) the great cost of the wars of Charles V and Philip II.
(b) its failure to develop a strong industrial base.
(c) the smuggling activities of the Dutch, English, and others.
(d) all of the above.

(d) p. 264

13.-.21: Don Quixote, Sancho Panza, and the imaginary Dulcinea were literary creations of

(a) El Greco.
(b) Gaspard de Caligny.
(c) Miguel de Cervantes.
(d) Baruch Spinoza.

(c) p. 264

13.-.22: In the course of the Wars of Religion in France, Catholics found an ally in Spain while Protestants looked to

(a) Italy.
(b) England.
(c) Austria.
(d) none of the above.

(b) p. 266

13.-.23: The phrase "Paris is worth a Mass" was attributed to

(a) Henry of Navarre.
(b) Catherine de' Medici.
(c) Jean Bodin.
(d) Maximilien Sully.

(a) p. 266

13.-.24: The Edict of Nantes

(a) resulted in the withdrawal of Spanish troops from France.
(b) granted substantial civil liberties to the Huguenots.
(c) saw Catherine de' Medici grant the papacy great powers.
(d) ended the first phase of the Thirty Years' War.

(b) p. 267

13.-.25: The politiques maintained that

(a) a policy of religious toleration was the best for France.
(b) mercantilism as an economic policy would ruin France.
(c) the unlimited power of the papacy should be restored in France.
(d) in spite of French law, Catherine de' Medici should rule France.

(a) p. 267

13.-.26: Which of the following statements regarding the reign of Henry VIII Tudor is NOT true?

(a) He avoided committing large armies to the Continent.
(b) The enclosure movement brought economic relief for small farmers.
(c) His expenditures on wives, the court, and wars, bankrupted England.
(d) His parliament was more modern than similar continental bodies.

(b) p. 268

13.-.27: In dealing with their parliaments, both Henry VIII and Elizabeth I

(a) were frequently frustrated by the legislative branch's control of new taxes.
(b) often found it necessary to use force to achieve their goals.
(c) usually got what they wanted without serious constitutional crises.
(d) were continually opposed by the gentry.

(c) pp. 268-270

13.-.28: Henry VIII Tudor was immediately succeeded on the throne by

(a) Mary Tudor.
(b) Edward VI.
(c) Elizabeth I.
(d) Mary, Queen of Scots.

(b) p. 268

13.-.29: A strong effort to reestablish the Catholic faith in England occurred under

(a) Elizabeth I.
(b) Edward VI.
(c) Mary Tudor.
(d) Lady Jane Grey.

(c) p. 268

13.-.30: Elizabeth I Tudor, on mounting the English throne, had a potentially dangerous rival in

(a) Anne of Cleaves.
(b) Catharine Parr.
(c) Mary Stuart, Queen of Scots.
(d) Mary Tudor.

(c) p. 269

13.-.31: The Thirty-Nine Articles, designed to resolve religious questions in England, was opposed by the

(a) Puritans.
(b) Presbyterians.
(c) Brownists.
(d) all of the above.

(d) p. 269

13.-.32: Which of the following was a major literary figure in the English Renaissance?

(a) Cervantes
(b) Sully
(c) Shakespeare
(d) Byron

(c) p. 271

13.-.33: During the last years of Elizabeth I's reign, a revolt led by the earl of Tyrone foreshadowed a long enduring conflict between England and

(a) Scotland.
(b) Wales.
(c) Ireland.
(d) all of the above.

(c) p. 270

13.-.34: The Dutch expanded the agricultural acreage through the creation of polders, which were

(a) military colonies gained through the conquest of German lands.
(b) areas cleared by extensive deforestation.
(c) farm plots gained by diking and draining land from the sea.
(d) none of the above.

(c) p. 272

13.-.35: He advanced the view that in matters of religion all persons must have absolute freedom of conscience.

(a) Edmund Spenser
(b) Baruch Spinoza
(c) Jan de Witt
(d) William Gilbert

(b) p. 273

13.-.36: The Thirty Years' War began as a conflict between

(a) Habsburg Austria and France.
(b) the Stuarts and the Bourbons.
(c) Protestants and Catholics.
(d) Spain and England.

(c) p. 273

13.-.37: A number of European states that were involved militarily in the Thirty Years War: which of the following was NOT?

(a) Denmark
(b) Sweden
(c) Austria
(d) England

(d) pp. 273-276

13.-.38: His private army waged a brutal war on behalf of the German Catholics.

(a) Gustavus Adolphus
(b) Cardinal Richelieu
(c) Albert of Wallenstein
(d) Frederick of the Palatinate

(c) p. 274

13.-.39: In the years between 1635 and 1648 the Thirty Years' War became primarily a struggle between the

(a) Swedes and Austrians.
(b) Habsburgs and Bourbons.
(c) Spanish and English.
(d) Stuarts and Valois.

(b) p. 275

13.-.40: The Thirty Years' War was brought to an end by the

(a) Edict of Restitution.
(b) Peace of Westphalia.
(c) Battle of White Mountain.
(d) Treaty of Cateau-Cambresis.

(b) p. 276

13.-.41: In his *Novum Organum* he argued that the scientist must rely upon the "empirical faculty."

(a) William Gilbert
(b) Francis Bacon
(c) Johannes Kepler
(d) Simon Stevin

(b) p. 276

13.-.42: His work, *Philosophiae Naturalis Principia Mathematica*, advanced some of the great discoveries of the seventeenth century.

(a) Roger Bacon
(b) Robert Boyle
(c) Isaac Newton
(d) Francis Bacon

(c) p. 279

13.-.43: The word "soldier" is derived from a Latin word meaning "piece of money." (True) p. 259

13.-.44: In Spain, as elsewhere, the growth of absolutism was marked by persistent struggles against local centers of power. (True) p. 280

13.-.45: Under the mercantilistic theory, merchants were supposed to be liberated from government regulations. (False) p. 263

13.-.46: Describe the power struggle among the great dynastic monarchies during the sixteenth and seventeenth centuries. What was the role of Spain and the New World?

Of England and the Dutch? Of France and the Italian states? Of the German and Scandinavian states?

13.-.47: How did the nature of warfare change during the shift from the medieval to the modern world? What new weapons were being used? What was the role of religious ideology? What was the role of national patriotism? What were the roles of the traditional nobility and the common soldiers? What was the importance of money, as opposed to feudal obligations?

13.-.48: What were the major issues which brought about the Thirty Years' War, and how did the Peace of Westphalia deal with those issues?

13.-.49: How did the ideas of Copernicus, Galileo, Descartes, Newton, and others create a "scientific revolution" against traditional ideals? What were the roles of inductive and deductive reasoning? What place did God have in a universe which seemed so rational?

13.-.50: If the 1500's can be viewed as the "Spanish Century," how did England and the Dutch Republic rise to become important powers by the end of the sixteenth century?

TEST ITEM FILE

CHAPTER 14: EXPLORATION AND EXPANSION

14.-.1: Which of the following motivated Europeans to explore and expand overseas in the early modern era?

(a) a desire to bring Christianity to the "heathens"
(b) the quest for personal glory
(c) a need to control strategic areas
(d) all of the above

(d) p. 282

14.-.2: Which of the following people have the best documented claim to having "discovered" the New World before Columbus?

(a) the Phoenicians
(b) the Welsh
(c) the Norsemen
(d) the Irish

(c) p. 283

14.-.3: Western expansion after 1400 differed from earlier expansion in all of the following ways EXCEPT that

(a) it was the first time great oceans were crossed.
(b) it moved Westerners away from their concept of the "known world."
(c) it was slower and more concentrated.
(d) it extended Western influence around the world.

(c) p. 283

14.-.4: He began the Portuguese efforts to find an all-sea route to the Far East.

(a) Pedro Cabral
(b) Prince Henry the Navigator
(c) Bartholomew Diaz
(d) King John III

(b) p. 283

14.-.5: Sailing around the Cape of Good Hope, he reached Calicut on the Malabar Coast of India in 1497.

(a) Columbus
(b) Vasco de Gama
(c) Rene Caillie
(d) Vespucci

(b) p. 286

14.-.6: The Treaty of Tordesillas in 1494

(a) recognized English claims in North America.
(b) divided the newly discovered lands between Spain and Portugal.
(c) was the first European treaty entered into with the Chinese.
(d) saw the state of Muscovy lay claim to Siberia.

(b) p. 286

14.-.7: He built up the Portuguese trading empire in India and southeast Asia.

(a) Alfonso de Albuquerque
(b) Ferdinand Magellan
(c) Liuz de Cameos
(d) Giovanni da Verrazzano

(a) p. 286

14.-.8: As Europeans pushed overseas, the region which they were slowest in penetrating was

(a) Mexico.
(b) sub-Saharan Africa.
(c) India.
(d) southeast Asia.

(b) p. 286

14.-.9: At the time of the arrival of Europeans on the coast of Africa the central and southern regions of that continent were

(a) peopled by natives little above the neolithic cultural level.
(b) largely under the control of Islamic rulers.
(c) in the hands of politically complex tribal states.
(d) sparsely populated because of infertile soil and water shortages.

(c) p. 286

14.-.10: The most powerful rulers in India in the Age of Discovery were the

(a) Manchu.
(b) Mogul.
(c) Ottoman Turks.
(d) Ming.

(b) p. 287

14.-.11: The item which Europeans had to trade with the rulers of India that had the greatest appeal was

(a) opium.

(b) firearms and military expertise.
(c) new religious concepts.
(d) silk.

(b) p. 287

14.-.12: Which of the following was NOT one of the major castes in Hindu society?

(a) Kshatriya
(b) Brahmins
(c) Vaisya
(d) Hinayana

(d) pp.287-288

14.-.13: In 1644 China was conquered by an invader from north of the Great Wall, the

(a) Japanese.
(b) Brahmins.
(c) Manchus.
(d) Mahayana.

(c) p. 288

14.-.14: The element in Chinese society which was in charge of running the vast bureaucracy were the mandarins: these were

(a) the military elite.
(b) intellectuals trained in the literary and philosophical classics.
(c) a corps of professional bureaucrats drawn from the merchant class.
(d) none of the above.

(b) p. 288

14.-.15: Confucianism may be described as

(a) a religion devoted to mystical pursuits.
(b) a code of conduct placing emphasis upon military power.
(c) an ethical system of manners and morals.
(d) a religion seeking to show how to obtain salvation.

(c) pp. 288-289

14.-.16: A significant element in the European nations' contact with the Far East were the "factories," which may be described as

(a) military outposts from which conquest of territory was undertaken.
(b) centers for the missionary activities of western faiths.
(c) posts from which trade was conducted with the native populations.
(d) offshore floating barges where items were manufactured.

(c) p. 289

14.-.17: Which of the following statements regarding the impact of European culture upon non-European peoples of Asia is NOT true?

(a) in the sixteenth century the masses were
not greatly influenced
(b) the local upper classes monopolized most of the European trade goods
(c) many local natives served in the European-led military forces
(d) Christian missionaries won the most converts in the Islamic regions

(d) p. 290

14.-.18: The Portuguese lost most of their holdings in India and southeast Asia to the

(a) Spanish.
(b) Arabs.
(c) Dutch.
(d) French.

(c) p. 290

14.-.19: When explorers arrived in Africa, they discovered that native tribes had already established these two empires.

(a) North Africa and West Africa
(b) Luba and Lunda
(c) Medieval Ghana and Mali
(d) Konga and Kuba

(c) p. 286

14.-.20: A major factor leading Columbus to believe that Asia could be reached by sailing west was

(a) the earlier voyages of Magellan
(b) an error regarding the circumference of the earth
(c) information gained from the fisherman of Brittany
(d) none of the above

(b) p. 290

14.-.21: Today Columbus is a figure of some controversy because many consider him responsible for launching in the New World all of the following EXCEPT

(a) racism
(b) democratic revolution
(c) exploitation
(d) ecological imperialism

(b) p. 291

14.-.22: The first New World explorer to look upon the Pacific Ocean was

(a) Juan Ponce de Leon

(b) Vasco Nunez de Balboa
(c) Magellan
(d) Pedro de Alvarado

(b) p. 291

14.-.23: The "Southwest Passage," the way westward to the Spice Islands of Asia, was first discovered by

(a) Sebastian Cabot
(b) Alvar Cabeza de Vaca
(c) Pedro de Mendoza
(d) Ferdinand Magellan

(d) p. 292

14.-.24: The great empire of the Incas fell to the adventurer

(a) Hernando Cortes.
(b) Hernando de Soto.
(c) Francisco Pizarro.
(d) Pedro de Mendoza.

(c) p. 292

14.-.25: The term mestizos refers to

(a) the ruling Spanish class in the New World.
(b) the merchant class of Mexico.
(c) individuals of mixed European Amerindian descent.
(d) the enslaved natives of the New World.

(c) p. 293

14.-.26: A significant factor in the ultimate failure of the Spanish settlements in the New World to achieve unity in the modern era was

(a) the lack of centralized Spanish administration in the New World.
(b) the many independent states created by the conquistadores.
(c) the numerous geographical barriers.
(d) none of the above.

(c) pp. 292-294

14.-.27: At the top of the Spanish administrative hierarchy in its overseas territories was the

(a) viceroy.
(b) encomienda.
(c) audiancia.
(d) Inquisition.

(a) p. 292

14.-.28: Individuals of European descent who were born in the Spanish New World were called

(a) mestizos.
(b) encomiendas.
(c) creoles.
(d) Indios.

(c) p. 293

14.-.29: Called the "Father of the Indians," he devoted his energies to the protection of the indigenous people of the Spanish New World

(a) Bartolome de las Casas.
(b) Antonio Pigafetta.
(c) Henri Mouhoy.
(d) Francisco de Coronado.

(a) p. 294

14.-.30: In contrast to Spanish holdings in the New World, Portugal's holding in Brazil

(a) developed primarily as an urban society.
(b) was subjected to more interference from foreign rivals.
(c) saw less mixture of the races.
(d) all of the above.

(b) p. 294

14.-.31: English claims to territories in North America were based initially on the exploratory activity of

(a) Sir Humphrey Gilbert.
(b) John Hawkins.
(c) John Cabot.
(d) Roger Williams.

(c) p. 294

14.-.32: The Englishman Henry Hudson was the first explorer to

(a) successfully pass through the Northwest Passage.
(b) reach the headwaters of the Mississippi River.
(c) lay claim to territories in North America for Holland.
(d) establish an English settlement in the New World.

(c) p. 294

14.-.33: "Machu Picchu" is the name of a city built by the

(a) Africans.

(b) Incas.
(c) Chinese.
(d) Arabs.

(b) p. 294

14.-.34: The first successful permanent settlement in North America was at

(a) Jamestown, Virginia.
(b) Roanoke Island, North Carolina.
(c) Fort Christiana, Delaware.
(d) St. Augustine, Florida.

(a) p. 295

14.-.35: Which of the following statements regarding the settlement of English colonies in North America is NOT true?

(a) Maryland was founded in part as a haven for English Catholics.
(b) Pennsylvania absorbed what had once been a Swedish settlement.
(c) abundant cheap land tended to deter the rise of a colonial nobility.
(d) strong royal authority slowed the development of legislative bodies.

(d) pp. 295-296

14.-.36: The coureur de bois in French Canada were

(a) Jesuit missionaries.
(b) fur trappers.
(c) indentured laborers.
(d) Indian allies.

(b) p. 296

14.-.37: The territorial claims of France in North America were greatly expanded by the sieur de La Salle, who discovered

(a) Hudson's Bay.
(b) the Mississippi River.
(c) the Great Lakes.
(d) the St. Lawrence River.

(b) p. 296

14.-.38: Which of the following statements about French Canada is NOT true?

(a) It was long viewed as a real peril by the English colonies.
(b) The French were more active in missionary work than the English.
(c) Canada was primarily "a trading empire with military ambitions."
(d) It provided the French mother country with most of its sugar.

(d) p. 296

14.-.39: The Japanese folk tale in the textbook suggests that

(a) Japanese philosophy is completely different than that of the Europeans.
(b) Japanese believed that some people had only one eye.
(c) human differences are in large part merely a matter of point of view.
(d) all of the above.

(c) p. 297

14.-.40: By 1700 the stage was set in India for a decisive struggle between

(a) Spain and Portugal.
(b) France and Holland.
(c) England and France.
(d) England and Spain.

(c) p. 296

14.-.41: Although losing many of its colonial holdings, Holland maintained a firm hold on this region until the mid-twentieth century

(a) the Hudson valley.
(b) Madagascar.
(c) the Philippines.
(d) Indonesia.

(d) p. 297

14.-.42: The Dutch early established a settlement in Africa at

(a) Macao.
(b) the mouth of the Gambia River.
(c) the Cape of Good Hope.
(d) Mauritius.

(c) p. 297

14.-.43: Russia's penetration and conquest of Siberia was initially led by

(a) Cossacks.
(b) homeless peasants.
(c) missionaries.
(d) none of the above.

(a) p. 298

14.-.44: An extensive collection of the early accounts of explorers was collected and edited by Richard Hakluyt (True) p. 300

14.-.45: The conventional date for the end of the "Age of Discovery," 1779, was marked by the death of Captain James Cook in the Sandwich (or Hawaiian) Islands. (True) p. 301

14.-.46: Timbuktu was a major city of the Aztec empire. (False) p. 286

14.-.47: The African slave trade was begun by the Africans and Arabs and turned into a profitable enterprise by the Portuguese, Dutch, and English. (True) p. 298

14.-.48: Rivalries among the major powers of Europe hampered their overseas expansion. (False) p. 283

14.-.49: Generally speaking, educated Europeans during the late Middle Ages believed that the world was flat. (False) p. 290

14.-.50: Write an essay describing, with examples, how words and phrases like "age of discovery," "the known world," and even "civilization" can betray hidden biases when used to describe the encounters of Europeans and non-Europeans between 1492 and 1779.

14.-.51: Many Europeans set forth under sail from Europe to find a route to "the Indies." Write an essay describing what they meant by "the Indies," and what they actually found. Give examples from both Eastward and Westward movement.

14.-.52: Write an essay comparing and contrasting the growth and subsequent decline of the Portuguese, Spanish, and Dutch empires.

14.-.53: Compare and contrast the strategic significance of the British and French sea-borne empires on the one hand, the Russian land-based empire on the other.

14.-.54: Compare and contrast the responses to European colonization of three countries of Asia, Japan, India, and China. What circumstances permitted each to respond differently, and how have those differences contributed to the situations in those countries today?

TEST ITEM FILE

CHAPTER 15: THE PROBLEM OF DIVINE-RIGHT MONARCHY

15.-.1: Which of the following statements regarding le grand siecle --the seventeenth century-- is NOT true?

(a) France was dominant in the military, political, and cultural spheres.
(b) It has been called the "century of genius."
(c) It saw England torn by political and social unrest.
(d) It was a century of continuous economic expansion.

(d) p. 307

15.-.2: The meeting of the French Estates General in 1614 was significant because

(a) it was able to gain control of the king's right to collect taxes.
(b) no such meeting was held again until 1789.
(c) for the first time in history it elected a French king.
(d) the noble class of France worked in union with the third estate.

(b) 307

15.-.3: While he served as the real power in France, Cardinal Richelieu's paramount goal was

(a) to eliminate all Protestant sects from France.
(b) the establishment of the French throne as truly absolute.
(c) destroy the mounting power of the Protestant German states.
(d) the creation of an alliance of Catholic monarchs to oppose England.

(b) pp. 307-308.

15.-.4: The Fronde was essentially a

(a) revolt on the part of French peasants suffering from famine.
(b) religious revolt on the part of the Huguenots.
(c) power struggle between Mazarin and the privileged nobles of France.
(d) movement by France's middle class to control the Estates General.

(c) p. 309

15.-.5: "In the legislature, the people are a check upon the nobility, and the nobility a check upon the people. . . while the king is a check upon both. . ." This quotation describes the political situation

(a) in England after the Glorious Revolution.
(b) in the Dutch republic.
(c) under Louis XIV of France.
(d) in the Holy Roman Empire after the Peace of Westphalia.

(a) p. 323

15.-.6: A significant consequence of Louis XIV's revocation of the Edict of Nantes was

(a) an economic and military weakening of France.
(b) the migration of thousands of Huguenots to Canada.
(c) a war with the Protestant allies of the Huguenots in Germany.
(d) the Fronde.

(a) p. 312

15.-.7: The Jansenists were

(a) a puritanical movement within the Catholic Church.
(b) an extreme middle class faction in the Estates General.
(c) the agents of the papacy in France.
(d) the royal agents of the French king in the provinces.

(a) p. 312

15.-.8: The chief spokesman of mercantilism in France was

(a) Bossuet.
(b) Colbert.
(c) Le Tellier.
(d) Martinet.

(b) p. 313

15.-.9: Which of the following were concepts that a mercantilist would support?

(a) A nation must avoid dependency on others for imported goods.
(b) The nation's economy requires centralized planning.
(c) Guilds reduced the energies needed for a strong economy.
(d) All of the above.

(d) p. 313

15.-.10: Which of the following men was NOT involved in the important military advances that took place in France under Louis XIV?

(a) Louvois
(b) Racine
(c) Vauban
(d) Martinet

(b) pp. 314, 328

15.-.11: In seeking to establish France's "natural frontiers," Louis XIV's main military thrust was toward

(a) Italy

(b) Austria and Switzerland
(c) Germany and the Low Countries
(d) Spain

(c) pp. 314-315

15.-.12: England became an even more bitter foe of France following the ascension to the English throne of Mary, James II's daughter, and her husband,

(a) Prince Eugene of Savoy
(b) George I of Hanover
(c) William of Orange
(d) none of the above

(c) p. 314

15.-.13: The Grand Alliance of the eighteenth century was formed to prevent

(a) French seizure of German lands east of the Rhine.
(b) the assertion of Habsburg influence in Protestant Switzerland.
(c) the union of France and Spain.
(d) Prussian aggression against Holland.

(c) p. 315

15.-.14: The War of the Spanish Succession saw France lose this region in the New World to England.

(a) the Ohio Valley
(b) Florida
(c) Nova Scotia
(d) France's Caribbean islands

(c) p. 315

15.-.15: Which of the following was NOT one of the terms of the Treaty of Utrecht of 1713?

(a) The Bourbons were granted the throne of Spain.
(b) England won the *asiento*.
(c) The Elector of Brandenburg became king in Prussia.
(d) England acquired Quebec.

(d) p. 315

15.-.16: The *asiento* referred to the

(a) right to control the slave trade of Spain's New World holdings.
(b) claim to Gibraltar.
(c) claim of the Habsburgs to the throne of Spain.
(d) right of a woman to inherit the throne of the Habsburg empire.

(a) p. 315

15.-.17: While "Puritanism" encompassed a number of religious groups, its core was based on the doctrines of

(a) Blaise Pascal.
(b) Luther.
(c) Zwingli and Calvin.
(d) the Anabaptists.

(c) p. 317

15.-.18: James I Stuart came into conflict with his Parliament over which of the following?

(a) refusal to dismiss his chief Justice Sir Edward Coke
(b) permission for Catholics to conduct religious services in public
(c) efforts to wed his son to a Spanish princess
(d) open support of the Puritans

(c) p. 317

15.-.19: In 1628 the English Parliament passed the Petition of Rights ("the Stuart Magna Carta") which

(a) returned England to Catholicism.
(b) limited the amount of money spent on exploration.
(c) put significant constitutional limitations on the Crown.
(d) guaranteed the right of Parliament to meet annually.

(c) p. 317

15.-.20: The Solemn League and Covenant of 1638 was

(a) the militant arm of the Puritan sect.
(b) a union organized to defend Scottish Presbyterians.
(c) the army formed and trained by Oliver Cromwell.
(d) the military force of the "Cavaliers."

(b) p. 318

15.-.21: The Long Parliament was the institution during the English Civil War which

(a) supported the royal power of Charles I.
(b) selected Oliver Cromwell as "Lord Protector."
(c) put through a series of reforms diminishing royal power.
(d) carried out the Glorious Revolution.

(c) p. 319

15.-.22: The "purge" conducted by Colonel Thomas Pride resulted in

(a) the banishment of Charles I Stuart from England.
(b) the exclusion of many Presbyterians from the House of Commons.

(c) a severe defeat for the New Model Army at Marston Moor.
(d) the restoration of Charles II Stuart to the throne of England.

(b) p. 320

15.-.23: Charles I Stuart was brought to trial by the

(a) New Model Army.
(b) Rump Parliament.
(c) Solemn League and Covenant.
(d) Star Chamber.

(b) p. 320

15.-.24: The Navigation Act of 1651, enacted under Oliver Cromwell, was designed to

(a) weaken the hold of France on Canada.
(b) undermine the maritime trade of Holland.
(c) strengthen England's hold on Ireland.
(d) break the Spanish trade monopoly in South America.

(b) p. 320

15.-.25: The Protectorate of Oliver Cromwell might best be described as

(a) a theocracy.
(b) an absolute monarchy
(c) a military regime.
(d) a limited monarchy.

(c) pp. 320, 321

15.-.26: In the course of the Puritan Revolution, the concept of a form of communism was preached by the

(a) Roundheads.
(b) Diggers.
(c) Quakers.
(d) followers of Cromwell.

(b) p. 322

15.-.27: The Religious Society of Friends is better known as the

(a) Presbyterians.
(b) Puritans.
(c) Quakers.
(d) High Church of England.

(c) p. 322

15.-.28: The "spark" which ignited the Glorious Revolution was

(a) James II Stuart's signing of an alliance with France.
(b) the birth of a son to James II's second wife.
(c) the rebellion of the Duke of Monmouth.
(d) the Anglo-Dutch War of 1664-1667.

(b) p. 324

15.-.29: The lead in the revolt against James II Stuart was taken by the

(a) Whigs.
(b) Tories.
(c) Scots.
(d) peasantry.

(a) p. 324

15.-.30: The "Glorious Revolution" brought to the throne of England

(a) Queen Anne.
(b) George I of Hanover.
(c) William and Mary.
(d) Charles II.

(c) p. 324

15.-.31: The Bill of Rights of 1689 affirmed

(a) the essential principle of parliamentary supremacy.
(b) frequent meetings of Parliament.
(c) parliamentary control of the purse strings.
(d) all of the above.

(d) p. 325

15.-.32: The Act of Settlement of 1701

(a) divested the House of Lords' power to veto the laws of the Commons.
(b) stated that members of the House of Commons would receive pay.
(c) clearly indicated Parliament's power to make a king.
(d) all of the above.

(c) p. 325

15.-.33: The battle of Boyne, fought between the supporters of the "Old Pretender" and the English, further embittered England's relations with

(a) Scotland.
(b) Spain.
(c) the Irish.
(d) the Dutch.

(c) p. 325

15.-.34: Holding that man's life in a "state of nature" was "solitary, poor, nasty, brutish, and short," he advocated the all-powerful state.

(a) John Milton
(b) Jonathan Swift
(c) Thomas Hobbes
(d) Christopher Wren

(c) p. 326

15.-.35: The most controversial thinker of the seventeenth century, his views on pantheism found few supporters until the era of romanticism, a century later.

(a) Thomas Hobbes
(b) Baruch Spinoza
(c) Nicholas Boileau
(d) John Locke

(b) p. 327

15.-.36: Which of the following was NOT a leading French writer of the seventeenth century?

(a) Jean de La Fontaine.
(b) Georges de La Tour.
(c) Pierre Corneille.
(d) Jean Baptiste Moliere.

(b) p. 328

15.-.37: Baroque art of the seventeenth century has tended to be associated with

(a) the Catholic Counter-Reformation.
(b) the rising middle class.
(c) the anti-religious attitudes of the new scientists.
(d) all of the above.

(a) p. 328

15.-.38: Which of the following is NOT a characteristic of the baroque painting?

(a) unprecedented financial success for some artists
(b) the use of nonrepresentational abstractions
(c) realistic portrayals of society
(d) emphasis on size

(b) p. 328

15.-.39: The *Night Watch* and the *Anatomy Lesson of Dr. Tulp* were two of the best known works of this baroque painter.

(a) Paul Rubens
(b) Frans Hans

(c) Rembrandt Van Rijn
(d) Anthony Van Dyck

(c) pp. 330, 331

15.-.40: He was best known for his design of St. Paul's Cathedral in London.

(a) Sir Christopher Wren
(b) Thomas Hobbes
(c) Henry Purcell
(d) John Milton

(a) p. 330

15.-.41: The first important operas, creations of the baroque age, were written in

(a) Paris.
(b) Munich.
(c) London.
(d) Venice.

(d) p. 331

15.-.42: Which of the following was NOT a social trend in the seventeenth century?

(a) a renewed interest in and search for "witches"
(b) a marked slowing down in the population increase
(c) an enhanced position for women in relation to property
(d) a steady improvement in the laborers' standard of living

(d) pp. 332-333

15.-.43: It was Cardinal Richelieu's policy to deprive the Huguenots of both their political rights and religious freedom. (False) p. 307

15.-.44: Mercantilism, practiced by Colbert, was central to French economic policy. (True) p. 335

15.-.45: During the Interregnum, England was an absolute monarchy dominated by William of Orange. (False) p. 335

15.-.46: Write an essay analyzing the theory and practice of "divine-right" monarchy, noting the strengths and weaknesses of social and political governance under the system. Illustrate your essay with examples from seventeenth century France.

15.-.47: Write an essay describing the attempts of the Stuart dynasty to strengthen royal power in England. Contrast Stuart policies with those of the Tudors, and indicate why the Glorious Revolution, which ended Stuart rule, was considered "glorious."

15.-.48: Thomas Hobbes and John Locke each based their political philosophies on the theory of a "contract" as the basis of government. How did their theories differ from each other, and what were the implications of their theories for seventeenth century English politics?

15.-.49: Write a description of Baroque art, architecture, and music, illustrating your essay with at least one example from each field.

15.-.50: Historians argue that the seventeenth century was both a "century of genius" and a "century of everyman." Write an essay explaining this paradox. Be sure to mention both intellectual "greats" and beliefs of the common people, such as witchcraft.

TEST ITEM FILE

CHAPTER 16: THE OLD REGIMES

16.-.1: Which of the following statements regarding the Old Regimes of the eighteenth century is NOT true?

(a) Their economy was primarily agrarian.
(b) Serfdom in western European states had largely disappeared.
(c) The influence of the second estate remained substantial.
(d) The papacy was able to dominate politics in all the major European states.

(d) p. 337

16.-.2: The policy of cameralism present in some states was designed to

(a) establish more representative government.
(b) create more efficient state planning budgets.
(c) enforce the policy of conformity to the state religion.
(d) end serfdom within the state.

(b) p. 340

16.-.3: Hoping to solve the problem of France's large national debt, the brilliant financier John Law

(a) advocated sweeping tax reform.
(b) sought to end France's overseas expansion.
(c) abandoned the country's mercantilist policies.
(d) increased the realm's paper money backed by land and trade wealth.

(d) p. 340

16.-.4: The Mississippi Bubble and the South Sea Bubble showed that

(a) large fortunes could be made by prudent investing in overseas areas.
(b) royal courts of England and France were becoming commercialized.
(c) even large, government-related, investment companies could fail, seriously damaging private investors.
(d) joint stock companies backed by the government provided secure investments.

(c) p. 340

16.-.5: Which of the following contributed to advances in agricultural production in the eighteenth century?

(a) the introduction of new crops
(b) the enclosure movement
(c) the adoption of the four-year rotation system
(d) all of the above

(d) p. 341

16.-.6: The enclosure movement in England of the eighteenth century was designed to

(a) stimulate the growth of factories.
(b) strengthen the mining industry.
(c) increase and consolidate crop lands.
(d) expand lands available for yeoman farmers.

(c) p. 341

16.-.7: Under the domestic system in England

(a) factory workers were prohibited from joining unions.
(b) spinning and weaving of yarn and cloth was done in the worker's home.
(c) farmers expanded the use of crop rotation and fertilization.
(d) shipbuilding was made a state monopoly.

(b) p. 341

16.-.8: The first major advance in industrialization in England was made in

(a) railroad construction.
(b) textile manufacturing.
(c) coal mining.
(d) none of the above.

(b) p. 342

16.-.9: The policy of "salutary neglect" saw the British government

(a) drawn into conflict with Spain in the New World.
(b) surrender her possessions in the Caribbean to France.
(c) permit a great deal of freedom to her colonial governments.
(d) end her alliances with former continental allies.

(c) p. 342

16.-.10: He was considered England's first prime minister.

(a) Lord Townshend
(b) Robert Walpole
(c) William Pitt the Younger
(d) James Hargraves

(b) p. 343

16.-.11: Which of the following statements regarding English government and society in the eighteenth century is NOT true?

(a) The first Hanoverian monarchs favored the Whigs.
(b) Admittance to the professions was limited to the class of gentlemen.

(c) "Pocket boroughs" were evidence of widespread political corruption.
(d) Little contact between the business and gentry classes existed.

(d) p. 343

16.-.12: In eighteenth century France a major stronghold of power for the noble class was the

(a) Estates General.
(b) *parlements*.
(c) business world.
(d) third estate.

(b) p. 344

16.-.13: Elizabeth Farnesse, queen of Spain, sought to gain lands for her sons in

(a) the Holy Roman Empire.
(b) Poland.
(c) Italy.
(d) the Low Countries.

(c) p. 345

16.-.14: The Treaty of Westphalia in 1648

(a) extended Austrian influence in the Balkans.
(b) showed the Holy Roman Emperor's weakness in the German states.
(c) led to the partition of Poland.
(d) permitted Prussia to annex Luxembourg.

(b) p. 346

16.-.15: The goal of Emperor Charles VI's Pragmatic Sanction was to

(a) end Russian influence in Poland.
(b) strengthen the military.
(c) secure Habsburg control of the Kingdom of Naples.
(d) guarantee the succession of his daughter, Maria Theresa.

(d) p. 346

16.-.16: Which of the following was NOT a policy of the Great Elector of Brandenburg?

(a) the abolition of serfdom in his lands
(b) utilization of the Junker class in state service
(c) encourage religious refugees from other lands to come to his land
(d) strengthen his military

(a) p. 347

16.-.17: As a result of his victory in the Great Northern War, Peter the Great gained for his country

(a) control of the Black Sea.
(b) access to the Baltic Sea.
(c) territories in the Balkans.
(d) a port on the Mediterranean.

(b) p. 350

16.-.18: Russian society under Peter the Great saw

(a) a decrease in serfdom.
(b) religious freedom expanded.
(c) the Turkish threat ended.
(d) state service for nobles.

(d) p. 350

16.-.19: Before the close of the eighteenth century, this once important nation ceased to exist as an independent unit

(a) Prussia.
(b) the Ottoman Empire.
(c) Poland.
(d) Holland.

(c) p. 351

16.-.20: As it grew weaker, the European territories of the so-called "sick man of Europe" became a center of conflict between

(a) Prussia and France.
(b) Russia and Austria.
(c) Poland and Hungary.
(d) France and England.

(b) p. 351

16.-.21: The *liberum veto* greatly weakened the power of its monarchs to govern effectively.

(a) Holland
(b) Denmark
(c) Poland
(d) Prussia

(c) p. 351

16.-.22: The basic issue behind the War of Jenkins's Ear was the

(a) struggle between France and England for control of Quebec.
(b) Russian expansion into the very heart of Europe.
(c) trade and smuggling in Spain's New World colonies.
(d) the question of torture and human rights.

(c) p. 353

16.-.23: As a result of the "Diplomatic Revolution," the following countries became allies

(a) Russia and England.
(b) Prussia and Austria.
(c) France and England.
(d) Austria and France.

(d) p. 353

16.-.24: In the Seven Years' War, Frederick the Great expanded his territories at the expense of

(a) Louis XV of France.
(b) Maria Theresa of Austria.
(c) Leopold of Belgium.
(d) George I, Elector of Hanover.

(b) p. 353

16.-.25: The "black hole of Calcutta" was an incident of atrocity against the troops of

(a) France.
(b) India.
(c) England.
(d) Prussia.

(c) p. 354

16.-.26: Which of the following nations and dynasties is NOT properly matched?

(a) Habsburgs of Austria
(b) Hanoverians of England
(c) Hohenzollerns of Prussia
(d) Kornilovs of Russia

(d) pp. 346-355

16.-.27: During the Seven Years' War, which of the following nations switched sides?

(a) England
(b) Russia
(c) France
(d) Spain

(b) p. 354

16.-.28: The battle between Generals Montcalm and Wolfe on the Plains of Abraham determined

(a) Prussia's status as a great European power.

(b) the fate of France's American empire.
(c) the outcome of the War of the Austrian Succession.
(d) that the Stuart dynasty would never again rule England.

(b) p. 355

16.-.29: Spain, on the losing side at the end of the Seven Years' War, ceded to England

(a) New Orleans and Louisiana
(b) Bermuda
(c) East and West Florida
(d) Gibraltar

(c) p. 355

16.-.30: The War of the Austrian Succession was called by that name because

(a) Austria had successfully dominated Italy.
(b) Prussia tried to forcibly convert Austria to Protestantism
(c) Several dynasties tried to prevent Maria Theresa from succeeding to the lands of her father.
(d) Russia and Austria succeeded in undermining the authority of the Ottoman Turkish Empire.

(c) pp. 352-353

16.-.31: Madame de Pompadour was the mistress of Frederick the Great of Prussia. (False) p. 345

16.-.32: For several decades the Jacobites represented a severe threat to the hold of the Hanoverians on the English throne. (False) pp. 343, 353

16.-.33: Voltaire considered Peter the Great to be an "enlightened despot." (True) p. 349

16.-.34: Under Peter the Great, efforts were made to expand Russian contacts with western Europe. (True) p. 348

16.-.35: The Zemski Sobor was the Ottoman administrative office in charge of foreign affairs. (False) p. 348

16.-.36: Under Peter the Great, Russia emerged as a great power. (True) p. 356

16.-.37: In seeking to take possession of Silesia, the king of Prussia was violating the Pragmatic Sanction. (True) p. 353

16.-.38: George Washington fought for the British against the French in a preliminary battle of the Seven Years' War. (True) p. 353

16.-.39: The English prime minister who led his nation to victory in the Seven Years' War was William Pitt. (True) p. 355

16.-.40: Write an essay distinguishing among the "commercial revolution," the "agricultural revolution," and the early "industrial revolution" during the period of the Old Regimes.

16.-.41: What can one imply about the social structure of the Old Regimes from the pictures in the text? Consider especially the woman working at the spinning jenny, the men in Hogarth's print of English electioneering, Boucher's portrait of Louis XVI's mistress, and the caricature of Peter the Great clipping a beard of a Boyar.

16.-.42: Sometimes it is said that the balance of power is a system of diplomacy designed to maintain peace. Yet the eighteenth century was full of warfare. How does one reconcile these two statements?

16.-.43: Describe the growth of the power of Prussia from the age of Frederick William the Great Elector in the seventeenth century to the age of Frederick II the Great in the eighteenth century. What factors account for Prussia's successes during this period?

16.-.44: Peter the Great had as his goal "not only to bring new greatness to Russia, but also to accomplish the complete assimilation of European customs," wrote a Russian novelist. Write an essay assessing the degree to which this statement is correct.

16.-.45: In eighteenth century Europe, people referred to the "Polish question" and the "Turkish question." What problems were faced by these two large countries during that period, and how did the European powers "answer" the "questions"?

16.-.46: During the period 1739-1763 a "diplomatic revolution" took place in Europe, in which traditional alliances were broken and new alliances established. Trace the developments in this "revolution," indicating what was "revolutionary" in the terms of the age.

16.-.47: The history of diplomacy and war is often analyzed in terms of the "balance of power." Write an essay describing the shifting balance of power in central Europe as Prussia and Russia both became more powerful during the eighteenth century.

16.-.48: The balance of power during the eighteenth century was not limited to Europe. Write an essay combining your knowledge of North American and European history, showing how the balance of power shifted back and forth across the Atlantic in the War of Jenkins's Ear, the War of the Austrian Succession, and the Seven Years' War.

16.-.49: Write an essay comparing the political and social systems of France and England during the eighteenth century. To the contemporary observers, just prior to 1789, do you believe one country looked like it was headed for revolution and the other was not? Why or why not?

16.-.50: What was "old" in the Old Regimes and what was modern and forward-looking? Write an essay addressing that question bringing in evidence from England, France, Russia and Prussia.

TEST ITEM FILE

CHAPTER 17: THE ENLIGHTENMENT

17.-.1: Which of the following was NOT one of those men of the "century of genius" who contributed to the basic principles of the philosophes?

(a) Rene Descartes
(b) John Calvin
(c) John Locke
(d) Isaac Newton

(b) p. 357

17.-.2: Denying the existence of innate ideas, it advanced the concept of the mind as a tabula rasa, a blank tablet upon which experiences wrote.

(a) Condorcet's The Progress of the Human Mind
(b) Rousseau's Emile
(c) Plato's Republic
(d) Locke's Essay Concerning Human Understanding

(d) p. 357

17.-.3: The optimistic outlook of the philosophes regarding the perfectibility of man and society was expressed most clearly by

(a) Voltaire.
(b) the marquis de Condorcet.
(c) David Hume.
(d) the Baron d'Holbach.

(b) p. 358

17.-.4: Which of the following is NOT a major key word for the eighteenth century?

(a) reason
(b) religious faith
(c) natural law
(d) progress

(b) p. 358

17.-.5: The editor of the Encyclopedie was

(a) Choiseul.
(b) Carl von Linne.
(c) Denis Diderot.
(d) the marques de Pombal.

(c) p. 359

17.-6: Which of the following concepts would NOT have been approved by Francois Quesnay and the Physiocrats?

(a) "Natural laws" exist which govern the economic sphere.
(b) The mercantilist concept of the accumulation of wealth is wrong.
(c) Rigid state regulation is necessary for its economy to thrive.
(d) True wealth is derived from agriculture.

(c) p. 359

17.-.7: The classical formation of laissez-faire economics was made by

(a) G.E. Lessing.
(b) Adam Smith.
(c) Tobias Smollet.
(d) John Wesley.

(b) pp. 360-361

17.-.8: Calling for reforms in his Essay on Crimes and Punishments, he held punishments should be clear, swift, and certain.

(a) David Hume
(b) Cesare Beccaria
(c) Jean-Jacques Rousseau
(d) Christoph Gluck

(b) p. 361

17.-.9: Which of the following statements about education in the age of the Enlightenment IS true?

(a) Diderot and Voltaire held leading university positions.
(b) The church had surrendered its role in education.
(c) Rousseau was a leading advocate of reform.
(d) all of the above.

(c) p. 361

17.-.10: It was the belief of the Deists that

(a) God, as the creator of the universe, existed.
(b) He was intimately involved in people's daily activities.
(c) good works, not prayer, were the best means of achieving grace.
(d) all of the above.

(a) p. 362

17.-.11: Voltaire's dedication to the idea of religious toleration was seen in his

(a) defense of the Society of Jesus against its critics.

(b) involvement in the affair of Jean Calas.
(c) support of Louis XIV's revocation of the Edict of Nantes.
(d) none of the above.

(b) p. 362

17.-.12: In Candide Voltaire raised the issue of the

(a) right of the common person to have a voice in government.
(b) the role of church in society.
(c) existence of disaster in "the best of all possible worlds."
(d) impact of technology upon society.

(c) p. 362

17.-.13: He saw the concept of checks and balances and separation of powers as a key to the superior structure of the British political system.

(a) Thomas Hobbes.
(b) Montesquieu.
(c) David Hume.
(d) Adam Smith.

(b) p. 362

17.-.14: Which of the following views would Rousseau have rejected?

(a) Individual self-interest may not oppose the "general will."
(b) Democracy is the form of government all nations should seek.
(c) The "general will" represents what is best for the whole community.
(d) The "social contract" involves all people in society.

(b) p. 363

17.-.15: Frederick II the Great of Prussia sought to achieve all but one of the following: which was NOT one of his goals?

(a) expansion of Prussia's agricultural and industrial production
(b) extending religious toleration to all but Jews
(c) breaking down the social class structure of Prussia
(d) improvement of the state's legal system

(c) pp. 364-365

17.-.16: "If a foreign country can supply us with a commodity cheaper than we ourselves can make it, better buy it of them . . . ." So wrote

(a) Adam Smith
(b) Frederick the Great of Prussia
(c) Cesare Beccaria
(d) the baron de Montesquieu

(a) p. 361

17.-.17: She introduced centralizing reforms in her realm, but banned the works of the major Enlightenment thinkers.

(a) Catherine the Great
(b) Madame de Pompadour
(c) Maria Theresa
(d) Elizabeth of Russia

(c) p. 365

17.-.18: Joseph II Austria attempted to

(a) reduce the number of monasteries in his land.
(b) free the serfs.
(c) pursue a policy of mercantilism.
(d) all of the above.

(d) p. 365

17.-.19: Which of the following rulers is NOT classified as an "Enlightened Despot"?

(a) Joseph II of Austria
(b) Leopold, grand duke of Tuscany
(c) Charles II of Spain
(d) Louis XV of France

(d) p. 366

17.-.20: Catherine the Great only instituted a few genuine reforms in Russia because she

(a) was born and raised in Germany.
(b) was too pious a Christian to accept Enlightenment ideals.
(c) was too dependant on the good will of the nobility.
(d) lacked the ambition to carry through on her ideals.

(c) p. 367

17.-.21: The activities of Yemelyan Pugachev of Russia

(a) led to the extension of Russian territory into Siberia
(b) led Catherine the Great to tighten controls on the local government.
(c) reflected the influence of the American Revolution in Russia.
(d) forced Catherine to abandon her policy of religious toleration.

(b) p. 368

17.-.22: This man's program of reform, had Alexander I enacted it, would have created a limited monarchy in Russia.

(a) Count Alexander Aracheev
(b) Stanislas Poniatowski

(c) Michael Speransky
(d) Yemelyan Pugachev

(c) p. 368

17.-.23: Catherine the Great sought to accomplish all of the following EXCEPT

(a) codify laws based on the ideas of the Enlightenment.
(b) reorganize local government.
(c) free the serfs.
(d) rule as an Enlightened despot.

(c) p. 368

17.-.24: Under Catherine the Great, Russia gained extensive and important territories at the expense of

(a) China.
(b) Poland.
(c) Austria.
(d) Sweden.

(b) p. 371

17.-.25: A strong and vocal opponent of George III in England's House of Commons was

(a) John Wilkes.
(b) David Hume.
(c) Lord Bute.
(d) John Locke.

(a) p. 370

17.-.26: Which of the following actions on the part of the British government did NOT occur in the period immediately following the Seven Years' War?

(a) Colonial settlers were prohibited from moving into the Ohio Valley.
(b) The policy of "salutary neglect" was gradually abandoned.
(c) Colonists were permitted laissez-faire trade to stimulate development.
(d) Parliament determined to raise greater revenues in the colonies.

(c) pp. 370-372

17.-.27: The victory won by the American rebels in this battle convinced the French to enter the Revolution on the colonial's side.

(a) Monmouth
(b) Saratoga
(c) Yorktown
(d) Valley Forge

(b) p. 373

17.-.28: The influence of which of the following is NOT to be seen in the American Constitution?

(a) Montesquieu
(b) Jean-Jacques Rousseau
(c) John Locke
(d) the English Bill of Rights

(b) p. 373

17.-.29: A critic of concepts held by the philosophes, he advanced a historical interpretation of the state as an organism subject to growth and decay.

(a) Immanuel Kant
(b) Giovanni Vico
(c) Samuel Richardson
(d) Nikolas Zinsendorf

(b) p. 373

17.-.30: While accepting many doctrines of the Enlightenment, he still explicitly emphasized a moral law in the conscience implanted by God.

(a) David Hume
(b) Daniel Defoe
(c) Immanuel Kant
(d) Henry Fielding

(c) p. 373

17.-.31: The evangelical revival of the eighteenth century began in

(a) Germany, with Zinsendorf.
(b) France, with Voltaire.
(c) England, with Wesley.
(d) Poland, with Kosiusco.

(a) pp. 373-374

17.-.32: A bitter, satirical attack on the optimism of the philosophes was seen in Jonathan Swift's

(a) Emile.
(b) Moll Flanders.
(c) Candide.
(d) Gulliver's Travels.

(d) p. 374

17.-.33: Which of the following works is NOT associated with the correct author?

(a) La Nouvelle Heloise, Rousseau

(b) Robinson Crusoe, Daniel Defoe
(c) Tom Jones, Henry Fielding
(d) Sorrows of Young Werther, Lessing

(d) p. 375

17.-.34: His engravings provided a graphic view of the evils and vices of London society.

(a) William Hogarth
(b) George Romney
(c) Horace Walpole
(d) none of the above

(a) p. 375

17.-.35: Which of the following was NOT a major composer of the Enlightenment period?

(a) Handel
(b) Reynolds
(c) Mozart
(d) Bach

(b) p. 375

17.-.36 Although highly critical of the French monarchy, the Encyclopedie had supporters among high officials of the regime and nobles at court. (True) p. 359

17.-.37: Joseph II of Austria and Charles III of Spain instituted enlightened reforms. (True) p. 376

17.-.38: Unlike the Physiocrats, Adam Smith maximized the role of the state in economic affairs. (False) p. 361

17.-.39: In the course of the eighteenth century the Jesuits, the staunch defenders of the papacy, were banished in many Catholic states. (True) p. 365

17.-.40: Jean-Jacques Rousseau has been held by scholars to have been one of the strongest foes of educational reform. (False) p. 361

17.-.41: What did it mean to be "enlightened," or to be an advocate of the "age of reason?" What was potentially revolutionary about this philosophy?

17.-.42: Write an essay considering the ideas of philosophes like Voltaire and Diderot. What did they contribute to the movement we call the Enlightenment?

17.-.43: "The French are generally considered to be among the leaders of the Enlightenment." Write an essay assessing the accuracy of that statement.

17.-.44: Compare and contrast the ideals and practices of Frederick the Great, renowned as an Enlightened Despot, and Maria Theresa of Austria, very much a traditionalist. p.

17.-.45: The Enlightenment, in theory and in practice, had substantial limitations; discuss them, with reference both to the importance of sensibility over pure reason and to the disinclination of monarchs and their civil servants to overturn politically entrenched traditions.

17.-.46: What ideas of "laissez-faire economics" differed from those of mercantilism? How could the concept of "laissez-faire" contribute to development of capitalism?

17.-.47: Consider the major Russian rulers from 1725 to 1825. To what extent did they express, or try to carry out, the ideals of the Enlightenment?

17.-.48: Write an essay considering the impact of Enlightenment ideas on the coming of the American Revolution. If George III had been an "enlightened despot," could he have avoided the revolution?

17.-.49: Not all eighteenth century writers and creative artists fit neatly into the rationalist ideals of the Enlightenment. Write an essay citing and describing some of them who did not.

17.-.50: "Today we are all, at the core, children of the ideals of the Enlightenment." Write an essay addressing that statement, noting specific ideals of the Enlightenment and the status of those ideas in Western Civilization today.

TEST ITEM FILE

CHAPTER 18: THE FRENCH REVOLUTION AND NAPOLEON

18.-.1: The immediate cause of the French Revolution was

(a) peasant violence.
(b) Louis XVI's scandalous lifestyle.
(c) France's financial problems.
(d) the Mississippi Land Bubble.

(c) p. 378

18.-.2: The most vocal class in French society calling for sweeping reforms was the

(a) bourgeoisie.
(b) clergy.
(c) military.
(d) peasantry.

(a) p. 380

18.-.3: Which of the following statements regarding the role of the clergy in the French Revolution is NOT true?

(a) It was in possession of significant French lands.
(b) The French taxpayers were angered by its exemption from taxes.
(c) The leading bishops lived simple lives, in keeping with their vows of poverty.
(d) The church performed many essential public functions.

(c) p. 379

18.-.4: The most influential element in the French government under Louis XVI tended to be the

(a) clergy.
(b) nobles of the sword.
(c) philosophes.
(d) nobles of the robe.

(d) p. 380

18.-.5: The long range causes of the French Revolution included which of the following?

(a) A conspiracy based in the Masonic lodges.
(b) The fact that France had not been ruled by enlightened monarchs.
(c) Napoleonic delusions of grandeur.
(d) All of the above.

(b) p. 378

18.-.6: Which of the following statements about the peasant class of France in 1789 is NOT true?

(a) A majority were still serfs.
(b) They suffered from over-population and land shortages.
(c) Their agricultural methods were generally backward.
(d) They did not demand the overthrow of the monarchy.

(a) p. 380

18.-.7: The sans-culottes were

(a) impoverished peasants.
(b) the urban working class.
(c) royal tax collectors.
(d) socialist revolutionaries.

(b) p. 380

18.-.8: The Assembly of Notables was called in 1787 to deal with the problem of

(a) serf revolts.
(b) Protestant unrest.
(c) taxes.
(d) widespread urban unrest.

(c) p. 381

18.-.9: Declaration of the Rights of Women was an influential pamphlet written by

(a) Count Honore Mirabeau.
(b) Mary Wollstonecraft.
(c) Olympe de Gouges.
(d) Marie Antoinette.

(c) p. 384

18.-.10: Those members of the Estates General who took the Tennis Court Oath swore to

(a) overthrow the monarchy.
(b) establish a republic.
(c) write a constitution.
(d) abolish established religions.

(c) p. 382

18.-.11: July 14, France's national holiday, commemorates the

(a) execution of Louis XVI.
(b) foundation of the First Republic.

(c) fall of the Bastille.
(d) Tennis Court Oath.

(c) p. 382

18.-.12: The "Great Fear" led to an outbreak of violence by the French

(a) industrial workers.
(b) Protestants.
(c) citizens of Paris.
(d) peasantry.

(d) pp. 382-383

18.-.13: Throughout the period of the Revolution, the city of Paris

(a) strongly supported the monarchy.
(b) acted as a moderate force.
(c) was the most revolutionary region.
(d) opposed the Jacobin faction.

(c) p. 383

18.-.14: The "Declaration of the Rights of Man" was a reflection of the social, political, and economic views of the

(a) middle class.
(b) nobles of the robe.
(c) church.
(d) Girondins.

(a) p. 383

18.-.15: Which of the following was NOT a consequence of the Civil Constitution of the Clergy?

(a) Virtual elimination of papal authority over the French clergy.
(b) Reduction of the number of bishops.
(c) Its overwhelming support by the French people.
(d) The election of bishops and priests as civil officials.

(c) p. 384

18.-.16: The Constitution of 1791 created a

(a) republic.
(b) democracy.
(c) constitutional monarchy.
(d) theocracy.

(c) p. 385

18.-.17: The "September Massacres" of 1791 saw the execution of

(a) the king and queen of France.
(b) the Committee of Public Safety.
(c) many alleged traitors and enemy agents.
(d) the "Thermidoreans."

(c) p. 386

18.-.18: The leading spokesman of the "Republic of Virtue" was

(a) Jacques Louis David.
(b) Maximilien Robespierre.
(c) Jacques Brissot.
(d) Georges Danton.

(b) p. 387

18.-.19: During the "Reign of Terror," power in France was in the hands of the

(a) Directory.
(b) Committee of Public Safety.
(c) National Assembly.
(d) Girondins.

(b) p. 387

18.-.20: The "Thermidorean Reaction" was inaugurated with the fall from power of

(a) the Directory.
(b) Maximilien Robespierre.
(c) the First Consul.
(d) Abbe Sieyes.

(b) pp. 389, 390

18.-.21: He is sometimes spoken of as the first modern communist.

(a) Condorcet
(b) Gracchus Babeuf
(c) Jean Paul Marat
(d) Lavoisier

(b) p. 390

18.-.22: The Concordat of 1801, negotiated by Napoleon, brought about a reconciliation between France and the

(a) Russian czar.
(b) Grand Alliance.
(c) papacy.
(d) French monarchists.

(c) p. 393

18.-.23: The activities of Francois Toussaint L'Ouverture and Jean Jacques Dessalines showed

(a) that Napoleon's troops were virtually unbeatable prior to 1812.
(b) French revolutionary ideas applied to people of color.
(c) the scientific method was furthered by the French Revolution.
(d) the negative effects of the Civil Constitution of the Clergy.

(b) p. 395

18.-.24: The significance of Lord Nelson's victory at Trafalgar was that it

(a) prevented Napoleon's conquest of Egypt.
(b) broke the alliance between France and Russia.
(c) drove the French army out of Spain.
(d) checked Napoleon's plans to invade England.

(d) p. 395

18.-.25: By the Treaty of Tilsit, Czar Alexander I

(a) joined the Grand Alliance against France.
(b) abandoned Russian claims on the Ottoman Empire.
(c) became Napoleon's ally.
(d) gained control of the Dardanelles.

(c) p. 395

18.-.26: The state most severely hurt by the Treaty of Tilsit was

(a) Prussia.
(b) Austria.
(c) the Ottoman Empire.
(d) France.

(a) p. 395

18.-.27: The basic goal behind the Continental System was the

(a) diplomatic isolation of Russia.
(b) economic weakening of England.
(c) union of France and Spain.
(d) unification of Germany.

(b) p. 396

18.-.28: Spoken of as a "deadly cancer" for Napoleon, the people of this land fought a bitter guerilla war against the French army

(a) Italy.
(b) Germany.
(c) Spain.

(d) Switzerland.

(c) pp. 396, 398

18.-.29: Which of the following was NOT associated with the growth of Prussian and German nationalism in the early nineteenth century?

(a) Gerhard von Scharnhorst
(b) Baron Karl vom und zum Stein
(c) J.G. Fichte
(d) Baron d'Holbach

(d) pp. 396-398

18.-.30: Napoleon's decision to invade Russia in 1812 was the result of

(a) Alexander I's growing political influence in the Balkans.
(b) Napoleon's frustration that he could not force Alexander I to abide by the Continental System.
(c) the seizure of the grand duchy of Warsaw by Russian forces.
(d) the establishment of an Anglo-Russian alliance.

(b) p. 398

18.-.31: Banished to the island of Elba, Napoleon returned to France in March of 1815, only to be defeated once again at

(a) the "Battle of the Nations."
(b) Borodino.
(c) Waterloo.
(d) Jena.

(c) p. 399

18.-.32: Napoleon spent his last days in confinement

(a) in the Bastille.
(b) under house arrest in Paris.
(c) on the British island of St. Helena.
(d) none of the above.

(c) p. 399

18.-.33: Which of the following was NOT a legacy of the French Revolution?

(a) the ideals embodied in the motto Liberte, Egalite, Fraternite
(b) greater economic opportunity for the middle class
(c) equal rights for French men and women
(d) the concept of the equality of all Frenchmen before the law

(c) p. 399

18.-.34: The efforts of King Louis XV of France to drastically alter the structure of France's parlements was directed against the peasants. (False) p. 379

18.-.35: The cahiers were lists of grievances related to the Old Regime drafted by the members of the third estate of France. (True) p. 381

18.-.36: Historians argue that the Civil Constitution of the Clergy was the biggest blunder of the Revolution. (True) p. 385

18.-.37: The efforts of the Directory to restore the French monarchy led to Napoleon's seizure of power. (False) p. 392

18.-.38: The Code Napoleon both ended slavery in all French territories and placed women on a basis of equality with men before the law. (False) p. 393

18.-.39: During the French Revolution the Girondins were more radical than the Jacobins. (False) p. 387.

18.-.40: The French Revolution significantly changed the lives of French peasants. (True) p. 399.

18.-.41: Write an essay comparing the French Revolution with the English Revolution of the 17th century. Can one argue that the French Revolution was more important, and more enduring than the English Revolution?

18.-.42: Describe the various social groups of the French Old Regime and the degree to which their discontents were causes of the French Revolution.

18.-43: Describe the various stages of the French Revolution, from the constitutional monarch, to the Terror, to the Directory.

18.-.44: What caused the French Revolution? Was it economic conditions? Was it the ideals of the Enlightenment? Did the two interact?

18.-.45: What was democratic about the French Revolution? And what was tyrannical or dictatorial? Address this question by discussing how Robespierre applied the ideals of liberty, equality, and fraternity.

18.-.46: Discuss the rise and fall of Napoleon Bonaparte, both from the standpoint of his personality and from the standpoint of political and military history.

18.-.47: What was the effect of the French Revolution on people of color in France and the French colonies?

18.-.48: During the period of the French Revolution and Napoleon French armies celebrated their greatest victories and their greatest defeats. How do you account for this paradox?

18.-.49: How did the Napoleonic wars contribute to the rise of nationalism in Germany, Russia, and Spain?

18.-.50: Assess the long-run impact of the French Revolution on the development of France toward a liberal democracy. What aspects of the French Revolution would you see as positive in this regard, and what aspects would you see as negative?

TEST ITEM FILE

CHAPTER 19: ROMANTICISM, REACTION, AND REVOLUTION

19.-.1: Which of the following was NOT a characteristic of Romanticism?

(a) Strong emotional ties with the medieval period.
(b) An emphasis upon the importance of the individual.
(c) Fascination with the grotesque and irrational.
(d) Strong rationalist and anti-clerical sentiments.

(d) p. 425

19.-.2: Which of the following was NOT a type of revolution affecting Europe in the period after 1815?

(a) industrial and economic
(b) religious
(c) intellectual and cultural
(d) political and social

(b) p. 408

19.-.3: The study of medieval literature and the theory of cultural nationalism, or Volksgeist, were stimulated by the works of

(a) Sir Charles Barry.
(b) Johann Gottfried von Herder.
(c) Jacques Louis David.
(d) Theodore Gericault.

(b) p. 406

19.-.4: Which of the following was NOT a composer of the Romantic age?

(a) Hector Berlioz
(b) Ludwig van Beethoven
(c) Carl Maria von Weber
(d) Alexander Pushkin

(d) pp. 406-408

19.-.5: The names of Constable, Turner, and Delacroix are closely associated with

(a) Romantic painting.
(b) the Congress of Vienna.
(c) the "poetry of protest."
(d) the Reform Bill of 1832.

(a) p. 408

19.-.6: An excellent example of the neoclassical in early nineteenth-century architecture is seen in the

(a) Pantheon in Rome.
(b) University of Virginia.
(c) English Houses of Parliament.
(d) Palace of Versailles.

(c) p. 409

19.-.7: The view of the historical process as one of conflict between a thesis and antithesis, with a resulting synthesis was advanced by

(a) G.W.F. Hegel.
(b) Edward Gibbon.
(c) Immanuel Kant.
(d) William Blake.

(a) pp. 408-409

19.-.8: Although an Englishman, Edmund Burke approved of the American Revolution because

(a) he hoped it would lead to the fall of the English monarchy.
(b) it was to him a reaffirmation of the English traditions of 1688.
(c) it stimulated the coming of the French Revolution.
(d) he saw the colonies as an economic burden to England.

(b) p. 410

19.-.9: Between 1809 and 1848, the political life of Europe tended to be dominated by

(a) Czar Nicholas I.
(b) Talleyrand.
(c) Prince Klemens von Metternich.
(d) Viscount Castlereagh.

(c) p. 410

19.-.10: At the Congress of Vienna the concept of the Holy Alliance, whereby all states would follow Christian teachings, was designed to

(a) end the slave trade.
(b) bring about disarmament for the great powers.
(c) save conservative governments from revolutions.
(d) liberate the Holy Land from the Turks.

(c) p. 411

19.-.11: The Congress of Vienna was almost disrupted over the issue of

(a) the Dardanelles.
(b) the Confederation of the Rhine

(c) Poland and Saxony.
(d) France's overseas colonies.

(c) p. 410

19.-.12: Which of the following was NOT one of the settlements reached at the Congress of Vienna?

(a) In theory the "sacred principle of legitimacy" was followed.
(b) Russia received Finland and Sweden got Norway.
(c) France was deprived of extensive lands once held by the Old Regime.
(d) Holland surrendered to Ceylon and the Cape of Good Hope to England.

(c) pp. 410-411

19.-.13: The announced goal of the Quadruple Alliance of 1815 was to

(a) halt the penetration of the Baltic states by Russia.
(b) secure the settlement reached by the Congress of Vienna.
(c) prepare for the division of the Ottoman territories in the Balkans.
(d) plan for a crusade against the Ottoman territories.

(b) p. 411

19.-.14: The Carbonari or "charcoal burners" played a significant role in the 1820 revolt in

(a) Spain.
(b) Naples.
(c) Russia.
(d) Portugal.

(b) p. 412

19.-.15: Talleyrand scored the greatest success of his long career at the Congress of Vienna because

(a) as a minor German prince, he blocked German unity under the Prussians.
(b) he convinced the victorious powers to accept France as their equal.
(c) as the minister of the King of England, he successfully protected the interests of the British Empire.
(d) as a former French Revolutionary, he convinced the Congress to adopt the ideas of liberte, egalite, fraternite.

(b) p. 410

19.-.16: "With the movements in this hemisphere we are of necessity more immediately connected, and by causes which must be obvious to all enlightened and impartial observers." Those words, by James Monroe, came in response to America's concern over

(a) European intentions to reconquer American colonies.
(b) French intervention in revolutionary Mexico.

(c) British efforts to crush the revolutions in Greece.
(d) the Decembrist revolt in Latin America.

(a) p. 413

19.-.17: Simon Bolivar led a revolutionary movement against the king of

(a) England.
(b) Portugal.
(c) Spain.
(d) France.

(c) p. 412

19.-.18: The Greeks won their independence from the Ottoman Turks through the military intervention of all of the following EXCEPT

(a) Russia.
(b) France.
(c) England.
(d) Austria.

(d) p. 414

19.-.19: In France the goal of the Ultra party was

(a) the overthrow of the monarchy and restoration of a republic.
(b) to undo the reforms that had been achieved in the Revolution.
(c) restore a member of the Bonaparte family to the imperial throne.
(d) extend political rights to the urban workers.

(b) p. 415

19.-.20: During the reign of Charles X of France the foundation of France's North African empire was laid with the capture of

(a) Algiers.
(b) Morocco.
(c) Libya.
(d) Egypt.

(a) p. 415

19.-.21: "Liberty at the Barricades" is a painting commemorating

(a) the Belgian revolution against the Dutch.
(b) a Roman rebellion against the pope.
(c) the revolutionary overthrow of Charles X in France.
(d) the doomed Decembrist revolt against the Russian czar.

(c) p. 414

19.-.22: While assuming the dress and manners of a well-to-do businessman, this ruler of the "July Monarchy" did little to expand democracy in France.

(a) Louis Philippe
(b) Charles X
(c) Louis XVIII
(d) Francois Guizot

(a) p. 415

19.-.23: The struggle of the Belgians for independence from Holland was successful in part because of the intervention of France and

(a) Prussia.
(b) England.
(c) Austria.
(d) Russia.

(b) p. 416

19.-.24: The Burschenschaft, a leading element in the revolutionary movement in the German states, was composed of

(a) urban workers.
(b) prosperous peasants.
(c) university students.
(d) veterans of the Napoleonic wars.

(c) p. 416

19.-.25: In the German area the Carlsbad Decrees were designed to

(a) bring about the unification of Germany.
(b) reaffirm the supremacy of the Protestant religion.
(c) enforce rigid censorship and curtail revolutionary activity.
(d) end serfdom.

(c) p. 416

19.-.26: The "lessons" of the revolutions of the 1830s indicated that

(a) they were only successful where they had active popular support.
(b) all of the established European powers opposed any revolutions.
(c) a people's desire for independence overrode existing class conflicts.
(d) all of the above.

(a) p. 548

19.-.27: The revolutions which swept Europe in 1848 had two common denominators, nationalism and

(a) class solidarity.
(b) socialism.

(c) liberalism.
(d) religious solidarity.

(c) p. 417

19.-.28: The revolutions of 1848 were inspired by

(a) a French attempt to reestablish the Napoleonic empire.
(b) nationalism and liberalism in central Europe.
(c) Czarist Russia's oppression of the serfs.
(d) Karl Marx's pamphlet, The Communist Manifesto.

(b) p. 418

19.-.29: By 1848 the regime of Louis Philippe found itself confronted with mounting opposition from

(a) republicans.
(b) socialists.
(c) Bonapartists.
(d) all of the above.

(d) p. 418

19.-.30: The national workshops, established briefly after the fall of the July Monarchy to relieve unemployment were the idea of

(a) Louis Blanc.
(b) Adolphe Thiers.
(c) Hector Berlioz.
(d) Francois Guizot.

(a) p. 418

19.-.31: The 1840s saw three movements competing for leadership in the Italian nationalistic movements: which of the following was NOT one of these?

(a) the Neo-Guelfs
(b) the Risorgimento
(c) Young Italy
(d) the Gironde

(d) p. 419

19.-.32: The romantic and liberal spokesman of Young Italy was

(a) Guiseppe Mazzini.
(b) King Charles Albert.
(c) Count Camillo Cavour.
(d) Pope Pius IX.

(a) p. 419

19.-.33: In the unsuccessful conflict which Italian nationalists waged for freedom from Habsburg domination, which of the following was NOT discredited?

(a) the Neo-Guelfs
(b) Young Italy
(c) Piedmont
(d) all of the above

(c) p. 420

19.-.34: Prussia's most solid contribution to German unification prior to 1848 was the Zollverein, which was

(a) a military high command to unify all German armies in case of war.
(b) an alliance of German states against possible French aggression.
(c) a customs union abolishing tariffs and tolls.
(d) a cultural organization emphasizing German musicians and poets.

(c) p. 420

19.-.35: The "Big Germany" versus "Little Germany" issue, which arose at the Frankfurt Assembly, centered upon the question of

(a) whether a unified Germany should be Catholic or Protestant.
(b) whether Austria should be included in a unified Germany.
(c) whether a unified Germany should adopt a republican form of government.
(d) whether the Prussian monarch should carry the title of "emperor."

(b) p. 420

19.-.36: In 1848 the Habsburg monarchy was confronted with rebellion on the part of all of the following EXCEPT

(a) the Magyars.
(b) the Italians of Lombardy-Venetia.
(c) the Czechs.
(d) the Swiss.

(d) p. 421

19.-.37: Lajos Kossuth was the leader of the movement on the part of these people in their struggle for independence from Habsburg rule.

(a) the Poles
(b) the Magyars
(c) the Swiss
(d) the Croats

(b) p. 421

19.-.38: The year 1848 saw the publication of

(a) The Communist Manifesto.

(b) <u>The Genius of Christianity</u>.
(c) <u>Hard Times</u>.
(d) <u>Ivanhoe</u>.

(a) p. 423

19.-39: Despite the ascendancy of counterrevolutionary forces after the defeat of Napoleon, the spirit of 1789 did not die in 1815. (True) p. 404

19.-40: At the heart of the Romantic movement was a rejection of the ideals of the Enlightenment. (True) p. 405

19.-.41: At the Congress of Vienna, the French were allowed no representatives to present their case. (False) p. 410

19.-.42: In 1848 major revolutionary movements arose and were defeated in England and Russia. (False) p. 424

19.-.43: Charles Dickens's view of nineteenth century England praised the domination of "fact, fact, fact." (False) p. 422.

19.-.44: "The modern age was ushered in by the Napoleonic Wars." Write an essay assessing the accurateness of that statement, considering both "pros" and "cons."

19.-.45: In what ways was the period 1815-1848 one of conservative reaction, and in what ways was it one of a struggle for liberty? Be sure to consider events of the 1820s, the 1830s, and the 1840s.

19.-.46: Why did Metternich and his supporters fear nationalism, and why did the nationalists consider themselves liberals?

19.-.47: Recount the major goals of the revolutionaries of 1848 and consider how and why they failed to achieve them. Describe the differences between the outbreaks in France, the German states, and the Italian states.

19.-.48: The period 1815 through 1848 was one of "romantic protest." Consider what was being protested against and who was doing the protesting. Was Romanticism a liberal, revolutionary, reactionary, or a conservative movement?

19.-.49: Describe the Congress of Vienna, its goals, its successes, and its failures. What part did the balance of power play in its approach to European diplomacy?

TEST ITEM FILE

CHAPTER 20: THE INDUSTRIAL SOCIETY

20.-.1: Which of the following was NOT a consequence of the industrial revolution?

(a) Urbanization accelerated.
(b) By 1900 a large majority of Europeans were industrial laborers.
(c) Pure science tended to give way to applied science.
(d) New tastes in art, literature, and music evolved.

(b) pp. 425-426

20.-.2: The initial developments in the industrialization of society occurred in

(a) the railroad industry.
(b) textile manufacturing.
(c) the area of chemical production.
(d) metallurgy.

(b) p. 427

20.-.3: The stages of industrialization moved from England throughout Europe until, by 1914, this country led in production of electrical goods.

(a) France
(b) Spain
(c) Germany
(d) the United States

(c) p. 427

20.-.4: Which of the following was NOT a factor in the lead England took in the industrialization of society?

(a) the geographical compactness of the British Isles
(b) significant deposits of the necessary minerals
(c) an ample reservoir of labor
(d) a decline in population

(d) p. 427

20.-.5: One of the most significant contributions of Eli Whitney to industrialization was the

(a) application of steam power to textile looms.
(b) development of assembly lines.
(c) concept of standardization and interchangeable parts.
(d) water-powered spinning jenny.

(c) p. 427

20.-.6: England's coal industry was stimulated to increase production by

(a) the need for coke in the iron industry.
(b) its domestic use in a land short of wood.
(c) its importance in producing steam power.
(d) all of the above.

(d) p. 428

20.-.7: Which of the following men did NOT contribute significantly to advances in the area of transportation in the nineteenth century?

(a) John McAdam
(b) George Stephenson
(c) Robert Fulton
(d) William Siemens

(d) pp. 428-429

20.-.8: In England, great financial stability resulted from the government policy of

(a) permitting numerous banks to issue banknotes after 1844.
(b) restricting the right of merchants to invest in the new industries.
(c) introducing the principle of limited liability.
(d) all of the above.

(c) p. 430

20.-.9: The first significant advance in the mechanization of agriculture was made by

(a) Justus Liebig.
(b) Henry Bessemer.
(c) Samuel Cunard.
(d) Cyrus McCormick.

(d) p. 430

20.-.10: In the second half of the nineteenth century, the English economy, which was the leader of the world, suffered from

(a) periods of prolonged inflation and depression.
(b) increasing agricultural stagnation.
(c) an increased tension between labor and management.
(d) all of the above.

(d) p. 430

20.-.11: As English agriculture declined, her role as the pioneer in scientific farming was taken over by

(a) Italy.

(b) France.
(c) Germany.
(d) Belgium.

(c) p. 431

20.-.12: While farming progressed and prospered in the nineteenth century as never before, this region suffered an agrarian depression.

(a) Canada
(b) France
(c) the United States
(d) Britain

(d) p. 430

20.-.13: An attack of "black rot" impacted on the potato crops here with disastrous social and economic consequences.

(a) Russia
(b) Germany
(c) Argentina
(d) Ireland

(d) p. 431

20.-.14: Which of the following statements regarding the impact of industrialization on society can be said with certainty?

(a) It led to a steady increase in the population.
(b) The living conditions of the working class were improved.
(c) Marked demographic changes occurred in terms of distribution of wealth.
(d) All of the above.

(d) p. 432

20.-.15: While most countries of Europe experienced a population explosion in the nineteenth century, the population here declined.

(a) England
(b) Germany
(c) Belgium
(d) Ireland

(d) p. 434

20.-.16: Which of the following statements regarding diseases in the nineteenth century is NOT true?

(a) Deaths from tuberculosis, diptheria and small pox were reduced.
(b) Overall mortality rates increased in Europe after 1850.
(c) Certain airborne diseases, such as influenza, tended to increase.
(d) Various childhood diseases, while still present, were less often fatal.

(b) p. 434

20.-.17: The English Reform Bill of 1832 represented a victory for the

(a) industrial worker.
(b) aristocracy.
(c) middle class.
(d) farm laborer.

(c) p. 435

20.-.18: In which of the following countries was universal manhood suffrage achieved only in the twentieth century?

(a) France
(b) Belgium
(c) Germany
(d) the United States

(d) p. 436

20.-.19: During the 1830s child labor in English factories was

(a) rare.
(b) frequent.
(c) forbidden.
(d) supervised by the state.

(d) p. 436

20.-.20: The precepts of "thrift, hard work and self-help" were his formula for laborers who wished to join the ranks of the middle class.

(a) Samuel Smiles
(b) David Ricardo
(c) Karl Marx
(d) Louis Blanc

(a) p. 437

20.-.21: Regarding social conditions in England during the era of industrialization, historians generally agree that

(a) the cost of food tended to increase markedly.
(b) the wages of skilled workers increased.
(c) job opportunities for women were rare.
(d) average housing conditions improved.

(b) p. 437

20.-.22: In his Essay on Population, he held that "population, when unchecked, increases in a geometrical ratio. Subsistence only increases in an arithmetic ratio."

(a) Charles Fourier
(b) Herbert Spenser
(c) Thomas Malthus
(d) Jeremy Bentham

(c) p. 437

20.-.23: The classical economists

(a) had an optimistic view of the world, believing in inevitable progress.
(b) believed in the overthrow of capitalism by the masses of the workers.
(c) believed that a beneficent God would assure a fair living for all workers.
(d) had a pessimistic view of prosperity for the common workers.

(d) p. 438

20.-.24: His utilitarian views held that the goal of the state should be "the greatest good for the greatest number."

(a) Karl Marx
(b) Georges Sorel
(c) Jeremy Bentham
(d) Auguste Blanqui

(c) p. 438

20.-.25: He established a Utopian socialist community at New Harmony, Indiana.

(a) John Roebling
(b) George Eliot
(c) Thomas Hood
(d) Robert Owen

(d) p. 441

20.-.26: His humanitarian liberalism criticized laissez-faire economics and called for women's rights.

(a) David Ricardo
(b) Robert Owen
(c) John Stuart Mill
(d) James Bruce

(c) pp. 438-439

20.-.27: "Organization, harmony, and industry," when combined with the Golden Rule, would give rise to the utopian society he envisioned.

(a) Saint Simon
(b) Thomas Malthus
(c) Karl Marx
(d) Mikhail Bakunin

(a) p. 440

20.-.28: Which of the following was NOT one of the three laws in history Karl Marx claimed to have discovered?

(a) class struggle
(b) economic determinism
(c) the inevitablity of communism
(d) the rise of imperialism

(d) pp. 442-443

20.-.29: Marx, as a prophet of the future, failed to take into consideration

(a) the strength of nationalism.
(b) that capitalism would correct its worst abuses.
(c) that the proletarians might assume the attitudes of the bourgeois.
(d) all of the above.

(d) pp. 442-444

20.-.30: The "revisionist" faction of the Second International parted with Marx on the issue of

(a) the desirability of the creation of a socialistic state.
(b) the actual depressed condition of the working class.
(c) the necessity of violent class struggle.
(d) all of the above.

(c) p. 444

20.-.31: An advocate of anarcho-syndicalism, he wrote Reflections on Violence.

(a) Charles Kingsley
(b) Georges Sorel
(c) Peter Kropotkin
(d) Friedrich Engels

(b) p. 444

20.-.32: "What is property?" he asked: his answer was "Property is theft."

(a) Joseph Proudhon
(b) Thomas Hood
(c) Houston Stewart Chamberlain
(d) Edward Blakely

(a) p. 445

20.-.33: The Syllabus of Errors of 1864 reflected the anti-liberal position of the

(a) Prussian state.

(b) English Tories.
(c) papacy.
(d) Social Darwinists.

(c) p. 445

20.-.34: Ideas advanced by Charles Darwin did NOT include

(a) that man is descended from apes currently in the wild.
(b) the concept of natural selection.
(c) in nature there is a process of "survival of the fittest."
(d) struggle for existence.

(a) p. 447

20.-.35: "Of man, as of all inferior creatures, the law by conformity to which the species is preserved, is that among adults the individuals best adapted to the conditions of their existence shall prosper most." This statement by Herbert Spencer reflected his belief in the views of

(a) liberalism.
(b) communism.
(c) socialism.
(d) Social Darwinism.

(d) p. 448

20.-.36: In The Passing of the Great Race, as well as in the writings of Arthur de Gobineau and Cecil Rhodes, which of the following concepts could be found?

(a) socialism.
(b) liberalism.
(c) racism.
(d) Christian Socialism.

(c) p.p.448-449

20.-.37: Holding that democracy is a system where the weak unjustly and unnaturally rule the world, he was a spokesman of nineteenth century elitism.

(a) Henri Bergson
(b) Friedrich Nietzsche
(c) Auguste Comte
(d) Honore de Balzac

(b) p. 450

20.-.38: His invention had a direct influence on the direction painting took in the second half of the nineteenth century.

(a) Gustave Eiffel
(b) Isaac Singer
(c) Louis Daguerre

(d) Samuel Smiles

(c) p. 452

20.-.39: Which of the following is an example of the remarkable painters of the late nineteenth century?

(a) Manet, whose "Picnic Lunch" mixed nudes with people in standard dress
(b) Monet, whose "Impression: Sunrise" gave rise to the term "impressionism"
(c) Cezanne, whose emphasis on geometric and architectural qualities exemplified postimpressionism
(d) all of the above

(d) pp. 452-453

20.-.40: Henry Bessemer's converter had a significant impact on coal mining technology in England. (False) p. 428

20.-.41: The Rothschilds' banking success developed from frequent and regular speculating on the European market. (False) p. 430

20.-.42: In making his predictions, Thomas Malthus failed to take into consideration the impact of science. (True) p. 437

20.-.43: Pope Leo XIII's Rerum novarum encouraged the establishment of Catholic trade unions. (True) p. 445

20.-.44: What was revolutionary about the Industrial Revolution? Discuss both the developments of new means of production and the impact of the new economic order on the lives of workers.

20.-.45: Describe how the industrial revolution came first to Great Britain, and how it went through the stages of industrial growth.

20.-.46: Compare and contrast the responses to industrialism by classical economists, Utopians, Marxists, and humanitarian liberals.

20.-.47: Describe and critique the theory of history set forth by Marx and Engels.

20.-.48: Describe and critique the theories of nineteenth century racism and elitism.

20.-.49: Write an essay showing the relationship between the ideas of Charles Darwin and the concepts of Social Darwinism.

20.-.50: Write an essay demonstrating the influence of the industrial revolution on painting and architecture in the ninettenth century. Be sure to mention Louis Daguerre, Claude Monet, the "Crystal Palace" and Gustave Eiffel.

TEST ITEM FILE

CHAPTER 21: THE MODERNIZATION OF NATIONS

21.-.1: Which of the following statements regarding the political life and society of nineteenth-century Europe is NOT true?

(a) The second half of the century saw nationalism strengthened.
(b) Competition among nations intensified.
(c) The pace of technological advance and influence leveled off.
(d) Societies often measured progress by the growth of literacy.

(c) p. 457

21.-.2: The belief that the world could be improved by human effort was known as

(a) nationalism.
(b) imperialism.
(c) meliorism.
(d) communism.

(c) p. 457

21.-.3: A basic argument advanced by Karl Marx was that

(a) the workers' revolution would erupt first in Russia.
(b) imperialism is the highest state of capitalism.
(c) the most revolutionary element in society is the peasantry.
(d) class is best understood in terms of the mode of production.

(d) p. 458

21.-.4: The coup d'etat of December 2, 1851, led to the fall of the Second Republic and his recognition as emperor of France.

(a) Archduke Maximilian
(b) Louis Napoleon
(c) Adolphe Thiers
(d) Marshal MacMahon

(b) p. 458

21.-.5: Which of the following was NOT an achievement of the French Second Empire?

(a) France's rise as Europe's leading producer of iron and steel
(b) extensive programs of urban renewal
(c) financial support by the state of private investments
(d) the expansion of railroads and industrial developments

(a) pp. 458-459

21.-.6: The foreign adventures of the Emperor Napoleon III involved the French people in conflict in all of the following EXCEPT

(a) Mexico.
(b) Russia.
(c) Great Britain.
(d) Italy.

(c) p. 459

21.-.7: The Paris Commune of 1871 was a

(a) Marxist uprising against the Second Empire.
(b) protest of Parisian radicals to France's defeat by Prussia.
(c) reaction to the Credit Mobilier scandal.
(d) movement by the Orleanists to restore the monarchy.

(b) p. 460

21.-.8: The Third Republic's political system was shown to be somewhat unstable by all of the following EXCEPT

(a) the activities of General Georges Boulanger.
(b) the Panama Scandal.
(c) the sale of Legion of Honor posts.
(d) the inefficient and corrupt French civil service.

(d) p. 462

21.-.9: Captain Alfred Dreyfus was ably defended against charges of treason by this writer.

(a) Emile Zola
(b) Georges Sand
(c) Georges Clemenceau
(d) Victor Hugo

(a) p. 463

21.-.10: To bring about the first stage of Italian unification, in 1859 Cavour won the military support of

(a) Prussia.
(b) Austria.
(c) England.
(d) France.

(d) p. 464

21.-.11: While contributing to the unification of Italy, it seemed briefly that this republican hero might clash with Cavour.

(a) Guiseppe Garibaldi

(b) Victor Emmanuel
(c) Georges Picquart
(d) Guiseppi Verdi

(a) p. 465

21.-.12: The so-called "Roman question" referred to

(a) Italian nationalists' desire to restore the ancient Roman Empire.
(b) Napoleon III's attack on Rome.
(c) the attempt of the pope to conquer and unify Italy.
(d) the annexation of the Papal States by the unified Italian state.

(d) pp. 465-466

21.-.13: Bismarck was able to provoke a war between Prussia and Austria over

(a) the Frankfurt parliament.
(b) the Carlsbad Decrees.
(c) Alsace-Lorraine.
(d) Schleswig-Holstein.

(d) p. 468

21.-.14: The question of the succession to the Spanish throne served as a factor contributing to a war between

(a) Italy and Austria.
(b) Spain and France.
(c) Prussia and France.
(d) Spain and Italy.

(c) p. 469

21.-.15: France's loss of this region in 1871 to Prussia created a desire on the part of the French for revenge.

(a) Normandy
(b) Schleswig-Holstein
(c) Alsace-Lorraine
(d) Luxembourg

(c) p. 469

21.-.16: The *Kulturkampf* saw Bismarck seek to weaken in Germany the influence of the

(a) Social Democrats.
(b) Catholic Church.
(c) Habsburgs.
(d) Reichstag.

(b) p. 469

21.-.17: The German Social Democratic Party was composed mostly of

(a) pragmatic leftists seeking to improve working conditions.
(b) anarchists seeking to assassinate the emperor.
(c) Catholic labor leaders seeking to improve the image of the church.
(d) nationalistic shopkeepers seeking German expansion.

(a) p. 470

21.-.18: Bismarck's fall from power came as a result of a clash with Emperor William II over

(a) Bismarck's policy towards the socialists.
(b) German relations with Russia.
(c) the methods by which executive decisions were reached.
(d) all of the above.

(d) pp. 470-471

21.-.19: Which of the following statements regarding the status of women in Germany in the late nineteenth century is NOT true?

(a) They were denied the right to vote.
(b) They were discouraged from advanced professional training.
(c) They were barred from the civil service.
(d) The few politically active women were usually linked with socialism.

(c) p. 471

21.-.20: Alfred von Tirpitz was a major figure in the

(a) development of German naval power.
(b) expansion of Marxism in Germany.
(c) establishment of German colonies in Africa.
(d) formation of the Russo-German alliance.

(a) p. 471

21.-.21: The naval and colonial policies pursued by Germany in the late nineteenth century led to mounting tension with

(a) the United States.
(b) Great Britain.
(c) Russia.
(d) Austria.

(b) p. 471

21.-.22: The Ausgleich (compromise) of 1867 was designed to resolve Austria's differences with the

(a) Russians.

(b) Magyars.
(c) Poles.
(d) Prussians.

(b) p. 474

21.-.23: Which of the following was NOT one of the national minorities that disturbed the calm of the Austro-Hungarian Monarchy prior to World War I?

(a) Jews
(b) Czechs
(c) Serbs
(d) Croats

(a) pp. 474-478

21.-.24: The Hungarian government attempted to destroy minority nationalism through a policy of

(a) socialism.
(b) collectivization.
(c) Magyarization.
(d) terrorism.

(c) pp. 475-478

21.-.25: The Zionist movement called for

(a) complete assimilation for Jews in Austria.
(b) the creation of a Jewish state.
(c) admission of Jews to the Russian Duma.
(d) relocation of Jews to Russia.

(b) p. 477

21.-.26: He provided a modest welfare program for Vienna, while catering to his followers' hatred of Jews, Marxists, and Magyars.

(a) Otto von Bismarck
(b) Alexander Bach
(c) Karl Lueger
(d) Klemens von Metternich

(c) p. 477

21.-.27: Unlike the situation in Austria, in Hungary anti-Semitism

(a) often became violent.
(b) was given official support by the Catholic church.
(c) never became an important political movement.
(d) was supported by an overwhelming majority of the population.

(c) p. 477

21.-.28: Social and political reforms in Russia in the nineteenth and early twentieth centuries normally came

(a) following the outbreak of terrorist activity.
(b) only when the Russian Duma acted.
(c) as a consequence of military setbacks abroad.
(d) when a regent ruled for an infant czar.

(c) p. 479

21.-.29: A firm policy of "Autocracy, Orthodoxy, and Nationality" within his state was followed by

(a) Bismarck.
(b) Nicholas I.
(c) Napoleon III.
(d) Francis Joseph.

(b) p. 479

21.-.30: The immediate cause of the Crimean War was

(a) a religious dispute in Palestine.
(b) Russian aggression in India.
(c) an uprising in Poland.
(d) the Austro-Turkish alliance.

(a) p. 480

21.-.31: A significant factor in the decision to end serfdom in Russia was

(a) Napoleon's invasion of Russia.
(b) fear of the spread of Marxist doctrines in the rural areas.
(c) the defeat suffered by Russia in the Russo-Japanese war.
(d) it had become an increasingly unprofitable institution.

(d) p. 480

21.-.32: In the mid-nineteenth century the Russian intelligentsia class tended to be divided into two main schools, the

(a) Marxists and Socialists.
(b) Slavophiles and Westerners.
(c) monarchists and republicans.
(d) none of the above.

(b) p. 482

21.-.33: All of the following were major Russian literary figures of the nineteenth century EXCEPT

(a) Anton Chekhov.

(b) Leo Tolstoy.
(c) Feodor Dostoevsky.
(d) Peter Stolypin.

(a) pp. 483, 486

21.-.34: An influential Russian revolutionary, he advocated violence together with "anarchism, collectivism, and atheism"

(a) Michael Bakunin.
(b) Mikhail Lermontov.
(c) Gregory Rasputin.
(d) Sergei Witte.

(a) p. 482

21.-.35: This philosophy maintained that it was necessary to smash all bonds holding the individual to the traditions of society.

(a) populism
(b) Slavophilism
(c) nihilism
(d) Zionism

(c) p. 482

21.-.36: Lenin's faction of the Russian Social Democratic party came to be called the

(a) Mensheviks.
(b) Socialist Revolutionaries.
(c) Bolsheviks.
(d) Constitutional Democrats.

(c) p. 484

21.-.37: Czar Alexander II was assassinated by members of the

(a) Zionists.
(b) Octobrists.
(c) People's Will.
(d) Kadets.

(c) p. 483

21.-.38: The Pale of Settlement was established by the Russian regime to

(a) create a military frontier against the Turks.
(b) serve as a region of exile in Siberia for terrorists.
(c) restrict the movements of the Jewish people.
(d) none of the above.

(c) p. 484

21.-.39: Count Sergei Witte was responsible for

(a) the extensive economic and industrial progress of Russia.
(b) convincing Czar Nicholas II to issue the October Manifesto.
(c) winning Russia favorable terms in the Treaty of Portsmouth.
(d) all of the above.

(d) pp. 484-486

21.-.40: The Russian Revolution of 1905 was sparked by "Bloody Sunday," an event which saw

(a) the destruction of the Russian fleet by the Japanese.
(b) hundreds of Russian workers killed by czarist troops.
(c) Nicholas II dissolve the Duma.
(d) the beginning of widespread pogroms in the Ukrainian region.

(b) p. 485

21.-.41: The "Union of the Russian People" and its militant arm the "Black Hundreds" directed their violence against the

(a) ministers of the czar.
(b) Russian Jews.
(c) aristocrats.
(d) members of the Duma.

(b) p. 486

21.-.42: Which of the following statements about the political and economic situation on the eve of the American Civil War is NOT true?

(a) Industrialization of the North was increasing.
(b) The economy of the South was based primarily on agriculture.
(c) Southern Democrats were losing political control of the nation.
(d) The North had a military advantage in its superior officer corps.

(d) p. 489

21.-.43: The Dreyfus Affair revealed a deep-seated anti-Semitism within French society. (True) p. 462

21.-.44: In the second half of the nineteenth century, French women laborers achieved equal status with their male counterparts. (False) p. 463

21.-.45: The imperialistic ambitions of Italy in Ethiopia suffered defeat by the Africans in the late nineteenth century. (True) p. 466

21.-.46: Russia's victory over Japan in the Russo-Japanese War opened the way for Russian penetration of Manchuria. (False) p. 484

21.-.47: Alfred Thayer Mahan was a leading spokesman of the importance of sea power in a nation's rise to greatness. (True) p. 492

21.-.48: Compare and contrast the developments toward a liberal and democratic nation-state in France, on the one hand, and Italy and Germany on the other between 1850 and 1914.

21.-.49: Describe the nationality problems in the Habsburg Empire between 1850 and 1914, including treatment of Italians and Germans as well as the Magyars, Jews, and Slavic peoples.

21.-.50: Write an essay analyzing the role of the "intelligentsia" in nineteenth-century Russia. Compare its role with that of the intellectual elites in Western Europe at the same period.

21.-.51: Compare and contrast the expansion of Russia and the expansion of the United States during the nineteenth century. Be sure to include geographical specifics and consideration of both idealism and force in your essay.

21.-.52: During the second half of the nineteenth century, Italy and Germany were united by military force and the United States was preserved by military force. Write an essay comparing these three countries' uses of force to achieve or maintain national unity.

21.-.53: Federal systems of government attempt to avoid some of the problems of tightly centralized governments on the one hand, and loose confederations on the other. Write an essay describing the United States federal system during the second half of the nineteenth century, indicating how it changed because of the Civil War. Why do you think such a federal system would not have worked for the Habsburg monarchy during the same period?

21.-.54: The word "imperial" was applied to the governments of Germany, France, Austria-Hungary, and Russia during all or parts of this period. What does the word indicate in each case?

21.-.55: "The modern history of the United States really begins with its entry into world affairs between 1898 and 1914." Write an essay assessing the accuracy of that judgement.

TEST ITEM FILE

CHAPTER 22: MODERN EMPIRES AND IMPERIALISM

22.-1: British power in the nineteenth century was based upon

(a) economic factors.
(b) the parliamentary system.
(c) the British navy.
(d) a combination of all of the above.

(b) p. 495

22.-.2: Between 1850 and 1900 23 million emigrants left Europe; 10 million of these came from

(a) France.
(b) Germany.
(c) Britain.
(d) Italy.

(c) p. 496

22.-.3: In nineteenth-century England, the center of political power was in the hands of

(a) the peers.
(b) the monarchy.
(c) Parliament.
(d) the trade unions.

(c) p. 497

22.-.4: Which of the following issues was NOT vital to women's movements in nineteenth-century Britain?

(a) the "Drink Question"
(b) the contagious disease acts
(c) universal suffrage
(d) the "Irish Question"

(d) p. 496

22.-.5: Which of the following was NOT a reform introduced in Britain in the 1820s?

(a) Laborers were permitted to organize unions.
(b) Reforms were undertaken in the criminal law code.
(c) Restrictions were removed on Catholics.
(d) All adult males were given the right to vote.

(d) p. 497

22.-.6: The Great Reform Bill of 1832

(a) gave seats in Parliament to forty industrial towns.
(b) gave about fifty percent of the working class the vote.
(c) strengthened the political power of the established church.
(d) all of the above.

(a) p. 498

22.-.7: The People's Charter represented the demands of the working class in Britain, including all of the following EXCEPT

(a) secret ballots.
(b) annually elected Parliaments.
(c) abolition of the monarchy.
(d) universal male suffrage.

(c) p. 498

22.-.8: The major figure in obtaining the enactment of the Reform Bill of 1867 was the Conservative leader

(a) William Gladstone.
(b) Benjamin Disraeli.
(c) Sir Robert Peel.
(d) George Canning.

(b) p. 499

22.-.9: He served as the leader of the Liberal Party of Britain in the late nineteenth century

(a) Lord Beaconsfield.
(b) William Gladstone.
(c) Lord Salisbury.
(d) Richard Cobden.

(b) p. 499

22.-.10: Which of the following statements regarding suffrage in England between 1885 and 1920 is TRUE?

(a) Women possessing property gained the right to vote.
(b) All adult males had the right to vote.
(c) There were some men in England who had plural votes.
(d) All of the above.

(d) p. 500

22.-.11: The goal of the Anti-Corn Law League was the

(a) liberation of England of its dependency on imported foods.

(b) adoption of a policy of free trade.
(c) prohibition of all alcoholic drinks.
(d) introduction of a policy of strict mercantilism.

(b) p. 501

22.-.12: The first member of the newly formed Labour Party to win a seat in Parliament was

(a) Kier Hardie.
(b) Richard Cobden.
(c) Michael Sadler.
(d) Benjamin Disraeli.

(a) p. 501

22.-.13: Which of the following was NOT a major piece of reform legislation in nineteenth-century Britain?

(a) New Poor Law
(b) Factory Acts
(c) Women's Suffrage Act
(d) 10 Hour Act

(c) pp. 500-503

22.-.14: The only European war in which British troops were actively involved between 1815 and 1914 was the

(a) Russo-Japanese War.
(b) Crimean War.
(c) Italian War of unification.
(d) Franco-Prussian War.

(b) p. 502

22.-.15: Joseph Chamberlain and his Unionist Party had as their major political plank

(a) protectionism in trade.
(b) opposition to the Boer War.
(c) the Irish question.
(d) unions' right to strike.

(a) p. 503

22.-.16: The "Peoples' Budget" of 1909 was introduced into Parliament by

(a) David Lloyd George.
(b) Thomas Arnold.
(c) Neville Chamberlain.
(d) Lord Shaftesbury.

(a) p. 503

22.-.17: To overcome the House of Lords' opposition to the Parliament Act of 1911, King George V threatened to

(a) abdicate.
(b) dissolve Parliament.
(c) create new peers.
(d) none of the above.

(c) p. 503

22.-.18: The goal of the Fabian Society was

(a) complete Irish independence.
(b) the achievement of social democracy through gradualism.
(c) abolition of the House of Lords.
(d) none of the above.

(b) p. 504

22.-.19: While a bill recognizing home rule for Ireland was enacted in 1912, it was never put into force because

(a) serious potato famine broke out in Ireland.
(b) Irish representatives were not permitted to sit in Parliament.
(c) strong opposition arose from the Irish province of Ulster.
(d) it was rejected by the English monarch.

(c) p. 505

22.-.20: He held that imperialism was the "highest stage of capitalism" and that capitalist states needed colonies as outlets for surplus capital.

(a) W.B. Yeats
(b) Beatrice Webb
(c) V.I. Lenin
(d) William Gladstone

(c) p. 506

22.-.21: Which of the following was a factor in the drive of European states to acquire colonies in the late nineteenth century?

(a) nationalism
(b) humanitarianism
(c) quest for strategic sites
(d) all of the above

(d) p. 509

22.-.22: "Take up the White Man's burden/ Send forth the best ye breed/ Go bind your sons to exile/ To serve your captives' need." So wrote the poet laureate of imperialism,

(a) Cecil Rhodes.
(b) Rudyard Kipling.
(c) Leander Jameson.
(d) W.B. Yeats.

(b) p. 508

22.-.23: Among the imperialist nations of Europe, which of the following steadily lost its holdings in the course of the 1800s?

(a) Germany
(b) Spain
(c) France
(d) Italy

(b) p. 509

22.-.24: The "Eastern question" centered on the

(a) fate of Islamic areas in the eastern Mediterranean.
(b) conflict between Japan and Russia.
(c) construction of the Suez Canal.
(d) the Muslim-Hindu conflict in India.

(a) p. 510

22.-.25: In 1914 only one of the following nations of Africa was not under the control of a European power: which one was NOT?

(a) Kenya
(b) Union of South Africa
(c) Abyssina
(d) the Congo

(c) p. 514

22.-.26: Japan, after years of seclusion, was opened in 1854 by

(a) Karl Peters.
(b) Evelyn Baring.
(c) Matthew C. Perry.
(d) Sir Alfred Milner.

(c) p. 511

22.-.27: The Durham Report led to full responsible government for this region.

(a) Upper and Lower Canada
(b) the Irish Free State
(c) Australia
(d) India

(a) p. 512

22.-.28: The Transvaal and Orange Free State were established by

(a) freed American slaves.
(b) Boers.
(c) refugees from Russia.
(d) Irish exiles.

(b) p. 513

22.-.29: At Khartoum he was slain by the troops of the Mahdi.

(a) Cecil Rhodes
(b) General Gordon
(c) Karl Peters
(d) Lord Cromer

(b) p. 516

22.-.30: The "Fashoda incident" in the Sudan saw a confrontation between

(a) Germany and Italy.
(b) France and Britain.
(c) Turkey and Italy.
(d) Britain and Germany.

(b) p. 516

22.-.31: It was frequently spoken of as the "Crown Jewel" of the British Empire.

(a) Australia
(b) Canada
(c) India
(d) Singapore

(c) p. 517

22.-.32: The rule of the British East India Company in India was ended in 1858 as a result of the

(a) Crimean War.
(b) Durham Report.
(c) Sepoy Rebellion.
(d) Boer War.

(c) p. 518

22.-.33: Which of the following North African regions was most closely linked to France politically?

(a) Tunisia
(b) Algeria
(c) Libya

(d) Morocco

(b) p. 519

22.-.34: Between 1904 and 1925 the United States intervened in which of the following states?

(a) Santo Domingo
(b) Haiti
(c) Nicaragua
(d) all of the above

(d) p. 523

22.-.35: Japan, in building its overseas empire, gained possession of Korea following a war with

(a) China.
(b) Russia.
(c) England.
(d) France.

(b) p. 523

22.-.36: In nineteenth-century British politics, there were great ideological differences between the Conservative and the Liberal parties. (False) p. 500

22.-.37: The English Liberal Party was badly split on the issue of Home Rule for Ireland. (True) p. 505

22.-.38: Beatrice Webb's definition of "socialism" included public education and public parks. (True) p. 504

22.-.39: Cecil Rhodes had a leading role in building Great Britain's African empire. (True) p. 515

22.-.40: British rule led to the failure of Indian economic development. (False) p. 518

22.-.41: Germany's efforts to gain colonial possessions were limited to only a few islands in the Pacific. (False) p. 519

22.-.42: The "new imperialism" after 1870 arose, in part, through the cooperation of indigenous leaders with the British and the French. (True) p. 509

22.-.43: In the aftermath of the Boer War with the British, South Africa became a self-governing dominion. (True) p. 515

22.-.44: Describe the development of British constitutional monarchy during the nineteenth century, from a parliamentary oligarchy to a democracy.

22.-.45: Write an essay defining "imperialism" in general and the "new imperialism" in particular, drawing examples from the British Empire.

22.-.46: Compare and contrast the empires of the major European states with those of the two major non-European states which developed empires during this period, the United States and Japan.

22.-.47: In the nineteenth century the British developed "dominion" status for Canada, and eventually extended it to other regions of the empire. Write an essay describing this "dominion" status, and explain why it was not applied to India prior to 1914.

22.-.48: Write an essay comparing the good effects and the bad effects of the New Imperialism upon the non-European world. On balance, would you say the non-Europeans benefitted from their colonial experiences?

22.-49: Write an essay on imperial policies regarding trade, slavery, and race. Select at least one example from each of the following empires: French, British, Dutch, Spanish, and Portuguese.

22.-.50: What was the relationship between the concepts of "imperialism" and "Western influence" during the late nineteenth and the early twentieth centuries? Give specific examples, drawing from the experiences of both Western and non-Western countries, such as Britain, Japan, India, and Australia.

TEST ITEM FILE

CHAPTER 23: GREAT WAR, GREAT REVOLUTION

23.-.1: The "spark" that ignited World War I was the

(a) German intervention in Morocco.
(b) sinking of the liner Lusitania.
(c) action of Gavrilo Princip in the city of Sarajevo.
(d) refusal of the Germans to honor the "scrap of paper."

(c) p. 529

23.-.2: Which of the following statements about public opinion on the eve of World War I is NOT true?

(a) Its tastes were reflected in the popular literature of the day.
(b) Opinion was often shaped by highly jingoistic press.
(c) Because newspapers were expensive, few could afford them.
(d) The press was at times used for political purposes.

(c) p. 530

23.-.3: Following the dismissal of Bismarck by the German emperor this nation was dropped from his alliance system.

(a) Austria
(b) Russia
(c) Italy
(d) England

(b) p. 531

23.-.4: In 1902 England concluded a formal alliance with

(a) Germany.
(b) Japan.
(c) the United States.
(d) France.

(b) p. 531

23.-.5: Which of the following states was NOT a member of the Triple Entente?

(a) Italy
(b) France
(c) Great Britain
(d) Russia

(a) p. 531

23.-.6: Which of the following was NOT a member of the Triple Alliance?

(a) Germany
(b) Russia
(c) Austria
(d) Japan

(b) p. 531

23.-.7: Relations between Great Britain and Germany were greatly strained as a result of

(a) Britain's alliance with the Ottoman Turks.
(b) German interference in the Sudan region of Africa.
(c) the Dreadnought race.
(d) Britain's colonial efforts in Malaysia.

(c) p. 532

23.-.8: Germany gave Austria a "blank check" in dealing with

(a) France.
(b) Turkey.
(c) Serbia.
(d) Russia.

(c) p. 533

23.-.9: Great Britain's entry into World War I came following the German invasion of

(a) Poland.
(b) France.
(c) Belgium.
(d) Russia.

(c) p. 532

23.-.10: The immediate cause of the United States entry into World War I was

(a) the rise of a communist regime in Russia.
(b) the decision of Italy to enter the war.
(c) the sinking of the Lusitania.
(d) Germany's resumption of unlimited submarine warfare.

(d) p. 534

23.-.11: World War I took the lives of how many soldiers?

(a) 800,000
(b) 1,000,000
(c) 8,000,000
(d) 36,000,000

(c) pp. 528, 535

23.-.12: The Schlieffen Plan, designed to quickly defeat the French, was thwarted at the battle of

(a) the Marne.
(b) Verdun.
(c) the Somme.
(d) Konigsberg.

(a) p. 536

23.-.13: The battles of Tannenberg and Masurian Lakes gained enduring fame for

(a) Brusilov.
(b) Foch.
(c) Hindenburg.
(d) Pershing.

(c) p. 536

23.-.14: A significant consequence of the defeat suffered by the Allies at Gallipoli was that

(a) it led the Ottoman Turks to enter the war.
(b) allowed Turkey to remain a German ally.
(c) Germany was in a position to close the Suez Canal.
(d) Italy was compelled to withdraw from the war.

(b) p. 537

23.-.15: The promise of "the establishment of a national home for the Jewish people" was given by the British in the Balfour Declaration, which was to be located

(a) in North Africa.
(b) in Palestine.
(c) in Eastern Europe.
(d) none of the above.

(b) p. 538

23.-.16: The battle Jutland, fought in the summer of 1916,

(a) saw Turkey knocked out of the war.
(b) was the battle fought by the Russian military in World War I.
(c) was the only major surface naval conflict of the war.
(d) saw American troops enter battle for the first time in the war.

(c) p. 538

23.-.17: Which of the following was one of the new weapons of war used in World War I?

(a) machine gun
(b) tank
(c) poison gas
(d) all of the above

(d) p. 539

23.-.18: The Amritsar Massacre in 1919 served to consolidate the nationalistic, anti-colonial feelings of the people of

(a) China.
(b) Russia.
(c) India.
(d) Ireland.

(c) p. 542

23.-.19: Which of the following was NOT one of the "Big Four" statesmen at the Versailles Peace Conference?

(a) Clemenceau
(b) Lenin
(c) Orlando
(d) Wilson

(b) p. 543

23.-.20: Karl Liebknecht and Rosa Luxemburg were leaders of the Communist party in

(a) Russia.
(b) Germany.
(c) France.
(d) the United States.

(b) p. 542

23.-.21: This British economist protested the harshness of the Treat of Versailles

(a) Clemenceau.
(b) Lord Grey.
(c) Keynes.
(d) Lloyd George.

(c) p. p. 543

23.-.22: The Polish Corridor, dividing this country territorially, would be a factor in the coming of World War II.

(a) Czechoslovakia
(b) Germany
(c) Austria
(d) Hungary

(b) p. 545

23.-.23: The "mandate" system was designed to

(a) prepare colonial peoples for eventual independence.
(b) organize the occupation of Germany by the allies.
(c) provide funds for rebuilding war-torn France.
(d) create a world government under the League of Nations.

(a) p. 545

23.-.24: Yugoslavia was established by the Versailles settlement in an attempt to unite

(a) Transylvania and Romania.
(b) the Czechs and the Slovaks.
(c) the Croats, Serbs, and Slovenes.
(d) Galicia, Estonia, and Bulgaria.

(c) pp. 544-545

23.-.25: which of the following was NOT a new nation that arose out of the break-up of czarist Russia?

(a) Estonia
(b) Latvia
(c) Romania
(d) Finland

(c) p. 545

23.-.26: Which of the following was a term imposed upon a defeated Germany by the Treaty of Versailles?

(a) the demilitarization of the Rhineland region
(b) acceptance of total "guilt" for the outbreak of World War I
(c) she could have neither submarines nor war planes
(d) all of the above

(d) p. 543-546

23.-.27: The U.S. Senate refused to join the League of Nations because it

(a) objected to the territorial provisions.
(b) treated the defeated powers too leniently.
(c) feared U.S. involvement in further European wars.
(d) was created by the Republican party.

(c) p. 546

23.-.28: Following the February/March Revolution, Lenin

(a) was sent into temporary exile.
(b) shared control of the ruling regime with Leon Trotsky.

(c) was returned to Russia by the German military.
(d) was released from prison in Siberia.

(c) p. 548

23.-.29: The February/March Revolution of 1917 in Russia saw control of the government pass briefly into the hands of

(a) Prince Michael Romanov.
(b) the military.
(c) the Soviet of Petrograd.
(d) a moderate provisional government.

(d) p. 547

23.-.30: Lenin believed that to be successful the revolution in Russia had to

(a) be controlled by a small, elite element of the Bolshevik Party.
(b) first go through a period of parliamentary democracy.
(c) disband the various "soviets" (councils) which had come into being.
(d) continue the war with Germany.

(a) p. 548

23.-.31: The leader of the Provisional Government in its final days was

(a) Lev Bronstein.
(b) Alexander Kerensky.
(c) Alexander Kolchak.
(d) Leon Trotsky.

(b) p. 549

23.-.32: The Provisional Government was severely weakened by a military coup attempted by

(a) Kornilov.
(b) Pilsudski.
(c) Baron Wrangel.
(d) Dzhugashvili.

(a) p. 549

23.-.33: The Constituent Assembly, elected by the Russian people in a democratic election,

(a) was unable to meet because of the advance of the German armies.
(b) selected Trotsky to arrange peace talks with the Germans.
(c) was disbursed at gunpoint by Lenin and the Bolsheviks.
(d) introduced the New Economic Policy.

(c) p. 551

23.-.34: The Bolsheviks agreed to accept the German peace terms in the Treaty of

(a) Lausanne.
(b) Brest-Litovsk.
(c) Sevres.
(d) Riga.

(b) p. 553

23.-.35: The possibility that the "workers'" revolution might spread to other nations of the world was seen in the activities of Bela Kun in

(a) France.
(b) Finland.
(c) Italy.
(d) Hungary.

(d) p. 542

23.-.36: The union of his nation in a federation with the Ukraine, White Russia, Lithuania, and Latvia was a vision of

(a) Baron Wrangler.
(b) Josef Pilsudski.
(c) Alexander Kolchak.
(d) Lord Curzon.

(b) p. 553

23.-.37: In 1921 Lenin successfully crushed a rebellion on the part of

(a) Finnish nationalism.
(b) Leon Trotsky.
(c) naval forces at Kronstadt.
(d) Joseph Stalin.

(c) p. 555

23.-.38: A literate population and mass newspapers made foreign policy a matter of public opinion. (True) p. 529

23.-.39: The Austrian government viewed Serbia as a threat that had to be severely punished. (True) p. 532

23.-.40: T.E. Lawrence was a strong opponent of the Arab nationalist movement of the World War I era. (False) p. 538

23.-.41: Propaganda played a significant role in the progress of World War I. (True) p. 534

23.-.42: World War I is considered a turning point in modern social history. (True) p. 540

23.-.43: The goals of Wilson's Fourteen Points included securing freedom of the seas and creation of a League of Nations. (True) p. 542

23.-.44: In spite of strong Republican opposition, President Woodrow Wilson was able to win Senate approval for the United States' entry into the League of Nations. (False) p. 546

23.-.45: The anti-Bolshevik White Russian forces received extensive military support from France in the Russian Civil War. (True) p. 554

23.-.46: The Treaty of Versailles assured the self-determination of all European peoples, including the Germans. (False) p. 543

23.-.47: Article 231 of the Treaty of Versailles clearly laid the blame for the war on German aggression. In retrospect, was that an historically accurate explanation of the cause of the war?

23.-.48: What impact did the Great War have on the home front in the various countries, both the victorious and the defeated? Can it be said that war, win or lose, creates revolution?

23.-.49: Compare and contrast Europe in 1914 with the Europe which was created by the Treaty of Versailles, including an outline map in the answer.

23.-.50: The Russian Revolution occurred in two phases, one in the spring and one in the fall. Consider why this was so, and the interrelationship between these phases and the war which was raging in Europe at the time.

23.-.51: We call the Great War by the name "World War I." To what extent was it really a "world" war, and what is the implication of the numeral?

TEST ITEM FILE

CHAPTER 24: BETWEEN THE WARS

24.-.1: Europe's "Age of Anxiety" between World War I and World War II was marked by

(a) political collapse.
(b) economic chaos.
(c) the spread and growth of fascism.
(d) all of the above.

(d) p. 557

24.-.2: The "fasci," from which the Fascists took their name were originally

(a) communists.
(b) elite troops in the World War I.
(c) Italian athletes.
(d) symbols of ancient Rome.

(d) p. 558

24.-.3: At various times in his career Mussolini was all of the following EXCEPT

(a) a socialist.
(b) a communist.
(c) a nationalist.
(d) a fascist.

(b) p. 558

24.-.4: The beginning of Mussolini's true dictatorship is said to have begun with the

(a) "march on Rome."
(b) corporative state's creation.
(c) invasion of Albania.
(d) murder of Matteotti.

(d) p. 560

24.-.5: In the corporative state of Italy, the nation in theory was governed by

(a) the military.
(b) the Fascist Grand Council.
(c) the Black Shirts.
(d) the Fascist Party.

(b) p. 560

24.-.6: In 1929 Mussolini settled Italy's long-standing conflict with

(a) Abyssina.
(b) the League of Nations.
(c) Yugoslavia.
(d) the papacy.

(d) p. 562

24.-.7: Which of the following was NOT an argument used against the Weimar Republic by its German foes?

(a) German efforts in World War I had been sabotaged by civilians.
(b) Aristocratic military leadership in the war had been poor.
(c) Its representatives had signed the Treaty of Versailles.
(d) It had accepted the "War Guilt" clause.

(b) p. 563

24.-.8: The threat of a communist revolution in Germany following World War I was seen in the

(a) Free Corps.
(b) Spartacists.
(c) followers of Ludendorff.
(d) Munich Beer Hall putsch.

(b) p. 563

24.-.9: As a consequence of the French occupation of the Ruhr in 1923

(a) the position of the Weimar Republic was strengthened.
(b) Hitler was able to seize control of Bavaria.
(c) the existing inflation went completely out of control.
(d) France and England reduced reparation payments.

(c) pp. 564-565

24.-.10: The concept of "Aryan" and "Nordic" supremacy was advanced by

(a) Gobineau.
(b) Rathenau.
(c) Marx.
(d) Ebert.

(a) p. 565

24.-.11: The book *The Foundations of the Nineteenth Century*, glorifying Germans and attacking Jews, was written by an

(a) Icelandic.
(b) Englishman.
(c) Italian.

(d) Austrian.

(b) p. 565

24.-.12: The able leader of Germany throughout much of the 1920s was

(a) Stresemann.
(b) Rathenau.
(c) Rosenberg.
(d) von Schleicher.

(a) pp. 565-566

24.-.13: The Young Plan resulted in

(a) the admission of Germany to the League of Nations.
(b) a substantial reduction in Germany's reparation payments.
(c) the foundation of the German air force.
(d) the rearmament of the Rhineland by the German military.

(b) p. 566

24.-.14: The SS (*Schutzstaffel*) is best defined as

(a) an organization of German veterans of the First World War.
(b) an elite guard of honor created by Hitler.
(c) a communist paramilitary force.
(d) the aristocratic officer corps of the German army.

(b) p. 567

24.-.15: Hitler became chancellor of Germany in 1933

(a) through the military force of the SA.
(b) because the Nazi party held a majority in the Reichstag.
(c) through appointment by President Hindenburg.
(d) by winning a majority of popular votes.

(c) p. 568

24.-.16: Hitler gained the Enabling Act, the basis of his dictatorial power, following

(a) a coup d'etat by the officers of the regular army.
(b) the burning of the Reichstag building.
(c) the destruction of the SA.
(d) an assassination attempt on his life.

(b) p. 568

24.-.17: The "blood purge" of 1934 saw the

(a) elimination of the SA as a factor in German politics.
(b) beginning of the "final solution."

(c) occupation of the Rhineland by German troops.
(d) annexation of Austria.

(a) p. 569

24.-.18: The Nuremberg Laws of 1935 were directed against the German

(a) socialists.
(b) Jews.
(c) businessmen.
(d) labor unions.

(b) p. 569

24.-.19: A leading exponent of "geopolitics," he influenced Hitler's theory of Lebensraum.

(a) Franz von Papen
(b) Heinrich Bruening
(c) Karl Haushofer
(d) Ernst Roehm

(c) p. 570

24.-.20: Hitler's Concordat of 1933 was an agreement between the Nazis and

(a) the Jewish community.
(b) the Vatican.
(c) Mussolini.
(d) Poland.

(b) p. 571

22.-.21: Mein Kampf was

(a) Lenin's blueprint for the conquest of the capitalist class.
(b) Hitler's political memoirs, written while in prison in the 1920s.
(c) a highly theoretical work of philosophy by Friedrich Nietzsche.
(d) none of the above.

(b) p. 565

24.-22: The leftist revolutionary movements in Spain tended to be most strongly influenced by the ideology of

(a) the Carlists.
(b) Bakunin and Sorel.
(c) Marx.
(d) the socialist revisionists.

(b) p. 572

24.-.23: The Spanish Republic, established in 1931, was quickly faced with a crisis over the issue of the

(a) status of the church.
(b) independence of the Basques.
(c) restoration of the monarchy.
(d) suppression of the socialists.

(a) p. 573

24.-.24: The party which General Francisco Franco established in power in Spain was the

(a) Carlists.
(b) Falange.
(c) Revolutionary Socialists.
(d) Constitutionalists.

(b) p. 573

24.-.25: In the course of the Spanish Civil War Franco received substantial military support from

(a) France and England.
(b) Italy and Germany.
(c) Russia.
(d) the United States.

(b) p. 573

24.-.26: "Guernica," a vivid and impassioned protest against the Spanish Civil War, was the work of

(a) Jose Antonio.
(b) Michael Karolyi.
(c) Pablo Picasso.
(d) Georges Sorel.

(c) p. 575

24.-.27: The Heimwehr and Schutzbund, private political armies, disturbed the peace of this land in the 1920s and 1930s

(a) Hungary.
(b) Danzig.
(c) Austria.
(d) Germany.

(c) p. 574

24.-.28: Kurt von Schuschnigg tried unsuccessfully to defend his country and prevent the Anschluss in the face of the aggression of

(a) Stalin.
(b) Hitler.
(c) Mussolini.
(d) Franco.

(b) pp. 574-575

24.-.29: Born after World War I, this country brought Serbs, Croats, and Slovenes together under one flag

(a) Hungary.
(b) Czechoslovakia.
(c) Romania.
(d) Yugoslavia.

(d) p. 576

24.-.30: The "Iron Guard," an anti-Semitic party, threatened the political stability of this land in the 1930s.

(a) Poland
(b) Romania
(c) Bulgaria
(d) Finland

(b) p. 576

24.-.31: Which of the following was Lenin's policy of economic reconstruction after the Civil War?

(a) the NEP
(b) War Communism
(c) the first Five Year Plan
(d) collectivization

(a) p. 577

24.-.32: Following Lenin's death, a power struggle occurred between Stalin and

(a) Sergei Kirov.
(b) Leon Trotsky.
(c) Maxim Gorky.
(d) Nikolai Bukharin.

(b) p. 578

24.-.33: The Great Purge in Russia of the 1930s was ignited by

(a) Sergei Kirov.
(b) Joseph Stalin.
(c) Leon Trotsky.
(d) the "Old Bolsheviks."

(b) p. 582

24.-.34: Once established in power, Mussolini quickly abolished the Italian monarchy. (False) p. 560

24.-.35: Ludendorff called for an armistice to end World War I because the German army, never defeated in the field, was "stabbed in the back" by revolutionaries at home. (False) p. 563

24.-.36: In 1923 Adolf Hitler sought unsuccessfully to overthrow the German government by a putsch in Bavaria. (True) p. 565

24.-.37: The assassination of President Hindenburg of the Weimar Republic paved the way for Hitler's rise to power. (False) p. 567

24.-.38: The state of Yugoslavia was politically unstable as a consequence of tensions between the Serbs and Croats. (True) p. 576

24.-.39: Following World War I the state of Austria was frequently torn by racial tensions. (False) p. 574

24.-.40: Stalin rose to power as Lenin's designated heir. (False) p. 578

24.-.41: The primary target of the movement to agricultural collectivization in the Soviet Union was the kulak class. (True) p. 580

24.-.42: As part of Stalin's purges, Leon Trotsky was assassinated in 1940. (True) p. 583

24.-.43: Modern technology played a significant role in the development of the "cult of personality" that surrounded the charismatic leadership of Hitler, Stalin and Mussolini. (True) p. 584

24.-.44: Among the "Ten Commandants for Fascists" was one which read "Mussolini is always right." (True) p. 561

24.-.45: Compare and contrast the dictatorships of Mussolini and Hitler on the one hand with that of Stalin on the other.

24.-.46: The United States fought the Great War to "make the world safe for democracy," and the U.S. won. Why, then, was democracy so strongly challenged in the 1920s and 1930s?

24.-.47: A number of smaller European states adopted and adapted the ideologies and practices of fascist leaders to their own countries. Using examples, discuss why they found these undemocratic approaches useful in their countries.

24.-.48: No dictator can take and maintain power by force alone in the modern world; there must be at least some attractive aspects to a regime for it to remain long in power. What was "attractive" in the regimes of Mussolini, Hitler and Stalin?

24.-.49: Write an essay accounting for the failure of Weimar Republic and the rise of Hitler to power. To what extent was Hitler's victory inevitable?

24.-.50: Describe the role that nationalism and racism played in both the ideologies and the practices of German Nazism and Soviet Communism.

TEST ITEM FILE

CHAPTER 25: THE DEMOCRACIES AND THE NON-WESTERN WORLD

25.-.1: Which of the following statements regarding Great Britain's economic status following World War I is NOT true?

(a) many of its overseas investments had been liquidated
(b) the United States, Canada, and Germany were strong industrial rivals
(c) it lacked manpower for the numerous industrial jobs peace created
(d) there was a sharp rise in the cost of living

(c) p. 587

25.-.2: During the inter-war years the democratic nations of France, Britain, and the United States were preoccupied by which of the following?

(a) domestic problems
(b) international crises
(c) economic problems
(d) all of the above

(d) p. 586

25.-.3: The nationalization of the key industries of Britain as the solution to that country's economic problems was advocated by the

(a) Conservatives.
(b) Labour Party.
(c) Liberals.
(d) MacDonald Coalition government.

(b) p. 588

25.-.4: The Statute of Westminster of 1931 resulted in the

(a) abdication of King Edward VIII to marry a commoner.
(b) creation of the British Commonwealth of Nations.
(c) partition of India and Pakistan.
(d) independence of the Union of South Africa.

(b) p. 589

25.-.5: His financial activities resulted in a scandal that severely shook the French political scene in the early 1930s.

(a) Leon Blum
(b) Serge Stavisky
(c) Raymond Poincare
(d) Edouard Daladier

(b) p. 590

25.-.6: The threat of fascism was seen in France in the activities of the

(a) CGT.
(b) Popular Front.
(c) Action Francaise.
(d) Cartel des Gauches.

(c) p. 590

25.-.7: The leader of the Popular Front in France was

(a) Edouard Daladier.
(b) Raymond Poincare.
(c) Leon Blum.
(d) Pierre Laval.

(c) p. 589

25.-.8: The first presidential election in the United States in which women could vote saw that office won by

(a) a Democrat.
(b) a Progressive.
(c) a Socialist.
(d) a Republican.

(d) p. 591

25.-.9: American isolationist attitudes were reflected in the 1920s by

(a) American activity as a member of the League of Nations.
(b) maintenance of a large army.
(c) higher tariffs.
(d) free trade with struggling countries of Asia.

(c) p. 591

25.-.10: Immigration policies in the United States during the 1920s favored the

(a) political refugees of southern and eastern Europe.
(b) Asian victims of Japanese aggression.
(c) people of northern Europe.
(d) Jews fleeing Nazi persecution.

(c) p. 591

25.-.11: Which of the following documents signaled the interest of the United States in world-wide peace by renouncing war as an instrument of national policy?

(a) Kellogg-Briand Pact.

(b) Treaty of Versailles.
(c) Nine Power Treaty.
(d) all of the above.

(a) p. 592

25.-.12: President Roosevelt's Social Security Act of 1935 helped U.S. citizens by creating benefits modeled after those of

(a) France.
(b) Germany.
(c) Spain.
(d) Great Britain.

(d) p. 595

25.-.13: Franklin Roosevelt called his program to rescue the United States from the Great Depression

(a) the Monroe Doctrine.
(b) My New Order.
(c) the Popular Front.
(d) the New Deal.

(d) p. 594

25.-.14: By the early 1930s political power in Japan was falling into the hands of the

(a) business leaders.
(b) leftist political factions.
(c) army and navy officers.
(d) Center Party.

(c) p. 597

25.-.15: The founder of the Kuomintang (Nationalist Party) of China was

(a) Huan Shih-kai.
(b) Sun Yat-sen.
(c) Chiang Kai-shek.
(d) Kang Yu-wei.

(b) p. 598

25.-.16: In 1915 this nation tried to make China a virtual protectorate by imposing on it the Twenty-One Demands.

(a) Russia
(b) Germany
(c) Japan
(d) the United States

(c) p. 598

25.-.17: In the 1920s Stalin did little to help the Communists of China because he

(a) feared it would antagonize the Japanese.
(b) felt that China was not ready for a proletarian revolution.
(c) personally opposed the Communist Party's leader Mao Tse-tung.
(d) believed it would lead to intervention by the United States.

(b) p. 598

25.-.18: Japanese aggression against China began openly in 1931 with the invasion of

(a) Korea.
(b) Manchuria.
(c) Formosa.
(d) Indochina.

(b) p. 599

25.-.19: The leader of India's Congress Party in its resistance to British rule was

(a) Ibn Saud.
(b) Satyagraha.
(c) Mustafa Kemal.
(d) Mohandas K. Ghandi.

(d) p. 600

25.-.20: In the inter-war years Arab nationalism tended to focus on the problem created by the

(a) Kellogg-Briand Pact.
(b) Locarno Treaty.
(c) Balfour Declaration.
(d) none of the above.

(c) p. 601

25.-.21: The Trade Disputes and Trade Union Act enacted in England in 1927 was a result of the fear of a communist coup. (False) p. 588

25.-.22: The Easter Rebellion won independence for the Irish Republic. (False) p. 589

25.-.23: The Sinn Fein Party sought the independence of Ireland. (True) p. 589

25.-.24: The "two Frances" of the inter-war years refers to republican France and communist France. (False) p. 590

25.-.25: The slogan "Better Hitler than Blum" reflected the anti-Semitic feelings of Austrian society in the 1930s. (False) p. 591

25.-.26: The Great Depression of 1929-1933 triggered many revolutionary movements in the United States. (False) p. 593

25.-.27: President Roosevelt's New Deal was designed to provide only immediate and short-term solutions to the Depression in the United States. (False) p. 594

25.-.28: Japanese women did not gain the right to vote until after World War II. (True) p. 597

25.-.29: The "Fists of Righteous Harmony," or Boxers, was a militant imperialist secret society in Japan in the 1920s. (False) p. 597

25.-.30: Great Britain was confronted with severe tensions between Zionists and Arabs in Palestine prior to World War II. (True) p. 600

25.-.31: Mustafa Kemal is sometimes spoken of as the "Father of Modern Iran." (False) p. 601

25.-.32: Describe the growth of democracy in the major countries of the West, noting how each built on the traditions of its own nation.

25.-.33: What did economic conditions have to do with the policies in the major countries of the West, both domestic and foreign?

25.-.34: What was the result of the Great War on the sense of colonial domination which had been felt by the major powers prior to 1914? And how were the colonies reacting?

25.-.35: During this period some countries maintained and enhanced democracy, while others lost it to authoritarian leaders. Why did democracy thrive some places and not others?

25.-.36: Write an essay describing the "Irish Question" between 1900 and 1939. How was the "question" answered?

25.-.37: Describe the political party structure of Britain between the wars, noting the differences between the Conservative and Labour parties.

25.-.38: Compare and contrast the "British Empire" and the "Commonwealth of Nations." Did the change to the Commonwealth indicate real progress, or was it only a cosmetic change?

25.-.39: Write an essay describing the political and economic impact of World War I on the France of the 1920s and 1930s.

25.-.40: Compare and contrast the response of Britain, France, and the United States on their respective post-World War I economic crises.

25.-.41: American policy during the interwar years is often described as "isolationism." Write an essay describing "isolationism," giving specific examples.

25.-.42: What was the American New Deal? Describe its strengths and its weaknesses.

25.-.43: Describe the impact of Japan, China, India, and the countries of the Middle East, on the policies of the Western Powers in the interwar period. Which of the non-Western areas was most influential?

25.-.44: Compare and contrast the Japanese Empire with the British Empire during the interwar period. Which was the more militarily aggressive?

25.-.45: How did the onset of the Great Depression affect the politics of Western Europe? Consider both the direct domestic impact, and the impact on foreign policies.

25.-.46: Consider the degree this history of the interwar period is basically "European history" and the degree to which it is basically "world history." Write an essay defending the proposition "European history in the interwar period is nothing without world history."

TEST ITEM FILE

CHAPTER 26: THE SECOND WORLD WAR AND ITS AFTERMATH

26.-.1: Which of the following was NOT an argument used by many Germans in their opposition to the terms imposed on Germany at Versailles?

(a) The normal rights of a state to arm itself were denied.
(b) Germany was stripped of territories and colonies.
(c) They wrongly held Germany solely responsible for World War I.
(d) They paved the way for the rise of communism.

(d) pp. 606-607

26.-.2: One explanation for the end of the "spirit of Locarno" was

(a) Mussolini's rise to power in Italy.
(b) the worldwide depression after 1929.
(c) Hitler's passage of the Enabling Act.
(d) Stalin's seizure of power in the Soviet Union.

(b) p. 607

26.-.3: The limitation imposed upon its naval armaments by the Washington Settlement of 1921-1922 angered

(a) Germany.
(b) the Soviet Union.
(c) France.
(d) Japan.

(d) p. 607

26.-.4: The attitude of many British politicians toward France in the 1920s was colored by their belief that France

(a) was dominated by leftist political factions.
(b) was seeking to establish its domination over Europe.
(c) was moving toward an alliance with the Soviet Union.
(d) might be taken over by a fascist regime.

(b) p. 607

26.-.5: An early indication of the weakness of the League of Nations to halt aggression was seen in 1923 in the

(a) Corfu incident.
(b) Anschluss.
(c) Japanese occupation of Korea.
(d) Soviet occupation of Finland.

(a) p. 608

26.-.6: The primary role of the Comintern of the Soviet Union was to

(a) stimulate anti-capitalist movements around the world.
(b) improve the agricultural production of the nation.
(c) rebuild the industrial capabilities of the nation.
(d) represent the Soviet Union in the League of Nations.

(a) p. 608

26.-.7: The "Zinoviev letter" resulted in strained relations between the Soviet Union and

(a) China.
(b) Poland.
(c) Great Britain.
(d) Nazi Germany.

(c) p. 608

26.-.8: A notable defeat for Stalin's foreign policy in the 1920s came in his relations with

(a) Germany.
(b) Finland.
(c) China.
(d) the Baltic Nations.

(c) p. 608

26.-.9: In the early 1930s the Soviet Union denounced which of the following as the most dangerous enemies of communism?

(a) Nazis of Germany
(b) Popular Front
(c) Social Democrats
(d) Conservatives of England

(c) p. 608

26.-.10: A secret protocol of the August 23, 1939, neutrality pact between the Soviet Union and Nazi Germany permitted

(a) Germany to occupy the Sudetenland of Czechoslovakia.
(b) the Anschluss.
(c) Soviet seizure of a portion of Poland.
(d) German use of Soviet naval bases in the Baltic Sea.

(c) p. 609

26.-.11: The Lytton Report of 1932 regarding Japanese activities in Manchuria was followed by

(a) the withdrawal of Japanese troops from that region.
(b) the imposition of harsh sanctions by the League of Nations.
(c) Japan's withdrawal from the League of Nations.
(d) the United States' promise of military support to Cuba.

(c) p. 610

26.-.12: Hitler's initial act in violation of the Treaty of Versailles saw him

(a) carry out the Anschluss.
(b) begin the rearmament of Germany.
(c) establish a non-aggresssion alliance with the Soviet Union.
(d) seize the Polish city of Danzig.

(b) p. 610

26.-.13: In 1935 he appeared before the League of Nations to appeal for help in his nation's struggle against the aggression of fascist Italy

(a) General Franco.
(b) Kemal Ataturk.
(c) Haile Selassie.
(d) Felix Eboue.

(c) p. 610

26.-.14: The Basque city of Guernica gained questionable fame when

(a) Hitler and Mussolini met there to sign the "Pact of Steel."
(b) German aircraft targeted its civilian population for savage bombing.
(c) the French army capitulated to the victorious German army.
(d) French and British diplomats agreed to the Anschluss.

(b) p. 610

26.-.15: Chancellor of this nation, Schuschnigg, was unable to prevent its occupation by the Nazi troops in 1938

(a) Poland.
(b) Austria.
(c) Czechoslovakia.
(d) Belgium.

(b) p. 611

26.-.16: Hitler's demands upon Czechoslovakia centered upon the issue of the

(a) city of Danzig.
(b) Maginot Line.
(c) Soviet-Czech Alliance.
(d) Sudeten Germans.

(d) p. 611

26.-.17: The Munich Conference of 1938, a sweeping victory of Hitler, exemplified the Western policy of

(a) balance of power.
(b) militarism.
(c) appeasement.
(d) none of the above.

(c) pp. 611-612

26.-.18: Hitler used the issue of the "Corridor" for his attack on

(a) Holland.
(b) Poland.
(c) Austria.
(d) France.

(b) pp. 612-613

26.-.19: Although losing early in the "winter war," eventually the Soviet Union's army defeated

(a) Japan.
(b) Yugoslavia.
(c) Finland.
(d) none of the above.

(c) p. 615

26.-.20: The so-called "phony war" came to a sudden end when Hitler launched a surprise invasion of

(a) Holland and Belgium.
(b) Denmark and Norway.
(c) Yugoslavia.
(d) France.

(b) p. 615

26.-.21: "Vichy France" was led by

(a) Paul Reynaud.
(b) Charles de Gaulle.
(c) Marshall Henri Petain.
(d) Edouard Daladier.

(c) p. 616

26.-.22: The "Battle of Britain" represented a significant defeat for the

(a) English communists.
(b) Afrika Corps.

(c) German Luftwaffe.
(d) British navy.

(c) p. 617

26.-.23: "I have nothing to offer but blood, toil, tears, and sweat." So spoke the World War II leader

(a) Winston Churchill.
(b) Charles de Gaulle.
(c) Joseph Stalin.
(d) Benito Mussolini.

(a) p. 615

26.-.24: Hitler's invasion of the Soviet Union was

(a) delayed by the stiff resistance offered by the Norwegians.
(b) delayed by German military involvement in the Yugoslavia and Greece.
(c) overshadowed by the "miracle of Dunkirk."
(d) welcomed by Stalin.

(b) p. 620

26.-.25: Which of the following regions did NOT fall to the Japanese armies in the early months of 1932?

(a) the Philippines
(b) Dutch Indonesia
(c) the Malay states
(d) northern Australia

(d) p. 621

26.-.26: Which of the following is NOT considered a "turning point" in the conflict between the Axis and Allied powers in World War II?

(a) the Battle of Stalingrad
(b) the Battle of El Alamein
(c) the Battle of Singapore
(d) the Battle of Midway

(c) p. 621

26.-.27: During World War II Mussolini

(a) was overthrown by the Italians but rescued by German commandos.
(b) fled to Berlin, where he perished in an Allied air raid.
(c) fled to Argentina.
(d) was captured by the Allies and was later executed.

(a) p. 623

26.-.28: The "Battle of the Bulge" marked the

(a) defeat of the German armies at Leningrad.
(b) last major offensive of the German armies of the western front.
(c) the Allied invasion of Sicily.
(d) the successful American landing in the Philippines in 1944.

(b) p. 624

26.-.29: The generally accepted number of Jews who perished in the Holocaust, the Nazis' "Final Solution," is

(a) five hundred thousand.
(b) two and a half million.
(c) between six and seven million.
(d) over ten million.

(c) p. 626

26.-.30: Which of the following nations was NOT designated a permanent member of the Security Council of the United Nations?

(a) the Soviet Union
(b) Great Britain
(c) the United States
(d) Japan

(d) p. 631

26.-.31: The Truman Doctrine was introduced in an effort to prevent a communist seizure of power in these lands.

(a) Spain and Portugal
(b) Greece and Turkey
(c) China and Japan
(d) Bulgaria and Hungary

(b) p. 632

26.-.32: Stalin suffered a defeat in his efforts to retain control over the communist regime of this nation.

(a) Poland
(b) Yugoslavia
(c) Czechoslovakia
(d) Romania

(b) p. 632

26.-.33: In 1956, when its leader Imre Nagy sought to follow policies that were independent of Moscow, the Soviet army crushed the "revolt" in this land.

(a) Hungary

(b) Poland
(c) Romania
(d) Yugoslavia

(a) p. 633

26.-.34: The U-2 incident ruined a projected summit meeting between the Soviet Union's Premier Khrushchev and President

(a) Johnson.
(b) Eisenhower.
(c) Kennedy.
(d) Truman.

(b) p. 634

26.-.35: In 1962 United States-Soviet relations seemingly reached the brink of war over Cuba when

(a) Khrushchev sought to introduce missiles into that nation.
(b) Fidel Castro overthrew the regime of General Fulgencio Batista.
(c) Cuban "volunteers" were discovered in Angola.
(d) none of the above.

(a) p. 634

26.-.37: Which of the following was NOT a factor leading to the Soviet-Chinese split?

(a) racial hatred on the part of the Soviets
(b) Soviet support of India in its conflict with the PRC
(c) Mao Zedong's decision to abandon Marxist-Leninist doctrines
(d) Khrushchev's efforts to raise the Soviet standard of living

(c) pp. 636-637

26.-.38: The Battle of Dien Bien Phu marked

(a) the final victory of Mao Zedong over the Chinese nationalists.
(b) France's final defeat in Vietnam.
(c) North Korea's invasion of South Korea.
(d) the destruction of Chinese communist influence in Indonesia.

(b) p. 638

26.-.39: The Cold War is now conventionally dated from the Berlin blockade in 1948 to 1989. (True) p. 641

26.-.40: The sinking of the American gunboat Panay provided evidence of the military aggressiveness of the Chinese Communists (False) p. 611

26.-.41: At the Munich Conference of 1938 there were no Czech officials present to represent their nation. (True) p. 611

26.-.42: The "miracle of Dunkirk" was in part due to Hitler's decision not to press the attack on the English forces. (True) p. 616

26.-.43: When the British and French realized that appeasement had failed to stop Hitler, they reluctantly sought a firmer alliance with the Soviets. (True) p. 609

26.-.44: A major commentator on American policy during the Cold War was George F. Kennan. (True) p. 635

26.-.45: Hitler, following Germany's defeat was tried and executed as a war criminal (False) p. 625

26.-.46: The Soviet Union took no part in the conflict against Japan in the Second World War. (False) p. 627

26.-.47: Yalta was the last major meeting of the Allied leaders in which President Roosevelt participated. (True) p. 628

26.-.50: In addition to demonstrating its power to the Soviet Union, some believe the U.S. decision to use the atomic bomb against Japan was also motivated by racism. (True) p. 627

26.-.51: Consider the long term and the immediate causes of World War II, both in Europe and in the Pacific. How do they relate to World War I?

26.-.52: Why did the Axis powers have the initial advantage in World War II, and how were the Allied powers able to turn the tide?

26.-.53: Describe the relationship between the USSR and the capitalist democratic states of the West before World War II, during the war, and immediately after. Was some sort of conflict predictable as soon as the Nazi threat was eliminated?

26.-.54: What was the place of the United States in the mid-twentieth century, and how does it differ from the U.S. place in the nineteenth and early twentieth centuries?

26.-.55: Write an essay describing the major turning points of the "cold war," from the tensions among the allied powers at the end of World War II to 1989.

TEST ITEM FILE

CHAPTER 27: TWENTIETH-CENTURY THOUGHT AND LETTERS

27.-.1: Which of the following pair of modern states has been most insulated against a comparative awareness of historical trends elsewhere?

(a) Great Britain and France
(b) the United States and the Soviet Union
(c) the United States and France
(d) the Soviet Union and Great Britain

(b) p. 644

27.-.2: The "father" of modern psychology was

(a) Alfred Adler.
(b) Marcel Duchamp.
(c) Sigmund Freud.
(d) Soren Kierkegaard.

(c) p. 647

27.-.3: The concepts of "collective unconscious" and "archetypes" were advanced by

(a) Max Weber.
(b) Carl Gustav Jung.
(c) Guilliaume Apollinaire.
(d) George Grosz.

(b) p. 648

27.-.4: The concepts advanced by Sigmund Freud have tended to reinforce the nineteenth century

(a) faith in the Darwinian concept of human progress.
(b) intellectual reaction against scientific materialism.
(c) faith in the rationality of man.
(d) belief in man's control of his actions.

(b) p. 648

27.-.5: Which of the following was NOT a prominent sociologist whose influence was greatest in post-World War II society?

(a) Vilfrado Pareto
(b) Max Weber
(c) Max Planck
(d) Emile Durkheim

(c) pp. 648-649

27.-.6: Logical positivists argue that human beings are at present

(a) incapable of persistent, successful logical thinking.
(b) capable of placing mind over matter.
(c) rational beings committed to following their own best interests.
(d) predestined to failure or to salvation.

(a) p. 649

27.-.7: A leading existentialist thinker, he argued that the individual does everything through choice and that absolute freedom exists.

(a) Edvard Munch
(b) Frederick Jackson Turner
(c) Robert Bechtel
(d) Jean-Paul Sartre

(d) p. 649

27.-.8: The impact of structuralism was felt in which of the following fields of study?

(a) anthropology
(b) history
(c) linguistics
(d) all of the above

(d) p. 650

27.-.9: The key creator of semiology was

(a) Claude-Gustave Levi-Strauss.
(b) Roland Barthes.
(c) Rudolf Carnap.
(d) Ludwig Wittgenstein.

(b) p. 650

27.-.10: According to this theory, the explanation of humanity's nature and destiny was in the absolutely determined course of dialectical materialism.

(a) structuralism
(b) Marxism
(c) existentialism
(d) none of the above

(b) p. 650

27.-.11: The Decline of the West was written by

(a) Karl Marx.

(b) Frederick Jackson Turner.
(c) Alexander Calder.
(d) Oswald Spengler.

(d) p. 650

27.-.12: He saw the rise and fall of civilizations as being determined by their ability to respond to challenges.

(a) Arnold Toynbee
(b) Leo Tolstoy
(c) Rudolf Carnap
(d) Walter Lippmann

(a) p. 650

27.-.13: He is held to have been the "father" of perhaps the greatest scientific event of the twentieth century.

(a) Bertrand Russell
(b) Albert Einstein
(c) Charles Beard
(d) Ludwig Wittgenstein

(b) p. 651

27.-.14: He is considered the founder of quantum physics.

(a) Max Planck
(b) Albert Einstein
(c) Werner Heisenberg
(d) Frederick J. Hoffman

(a) p. 651

27.-.15: He proposed the principle of indeterminacy, which held that scientists, in their study of the universe and matter, will have to be content with probabilities rather than absolutes.

(a) Ludwig Wittgenstein
(b) Charles Beard
(c) Murray Gell-Mann
(d) Werner Heisenberg

(d) p. 651

27.-.16: The discoverer of the "quark," perhaps the basis of all matter in the universe, was

(a) Murray Gell-Mann.
(b) Alexander Calder.
(c) Bertrand Russell.
(d) Ludwig Wittgenstein.

(a) p. 651

27.-.17: Within the rise of the environmental movement, he is considered the "father of ecology" because of his theory that every human act has a consequence in nature.

(a) Bertrand Russell
(b) Murray Gell-Mann
(c) Werner Heisenberg
(d) George Perkins Marsh

(d) p. 652

27.-.18: "This is the way the world ends / Not with a bang but a whimper:" in his work "The Hollow Men," he thus expressed the despair of an age.

(a) T.S. Eliot
(b) Albert Camus
(c) James Joyce
(d) William Faulkner

(a) p. 653

27.-.19: His controversial portraits of Dublin life, drawing upon the psychology of the unconsciousness, made him one of the most innovative twentieth-century novelists.

(a) Albert Camus
(b) James Joyce
(c) Thomas Mann
(d) William Faulkner

(d) p. 654
27.-.20: The best representative of the endless variety and experimentation of twentieth-century painting is

(a) El Greco.
(b) Pablo Picasso.
(c) Yves Tanguy.
(d) Olga W. Vickery.

(b) p. 655

27.-.21: An artistic protest movement in the years immediately after World War I was known as

(a) Dada.
(b) existentialism.
(c) historicism.
(d) impressionism.

(a) p. 656

27.-.22: His sculpture "Family Group" was completed between 1945 and 1949.

(a) George Grosz
(b) Jean Arp
(c) Henry Moore
(d) Jackson Pollack

(c) p. 656

27.-.23: Which of the following is NOT a twentieth-century sculptor?

(a) Henry Moore
(b) Andy Warhol
(c) Alberto Giacometti
(d) Barbara Hepworth

(b) p. 656

27.-.24: A leading innovator of modern architecture was

(a) Max Ernst.
(b) Alexander Calder.
(c) Marcel Duchamp.
(d) Frank Lloyd Wright.

(d) p. 658

27.-.25: One can no longer study Western civilization in isolation from the non-Western regions. (True) p. 643

27.-.26: Because the facts are available to the historian, it is difficult to manipulate history. (False) p. 643

27.-.27: In Freudian terminology, the id refers to a person's unconscious drives. (True) p. 646

27.-.28: Behavioralism influenced the study of political science, psychology, economics and medicine. (True) p. 649

27.-.29: Existentialism provides a negative picture of the human condition. (True) p. 649

27.-.30: The attempt to answer questions about the structure of the universe through history is called structuralism. (False) p. 650

27.-.31: The writings of Arnold Toynbee provide an example of historicism. (True) p. 650

27.-.32: Since the 1950s, historians have seen American society as a compilation of unalloyed success stories. (False) p. 650

27.-.33: One of the great environmental concerns of the late twentieth century is the problem of global warming and the greenhouse effect. (True) p. 653

27.-.34: The works of Andy Warhol are reflective of modern "pop-art." (True) p. 656

27.-.35: American pop music culture has had little impact on global popular culture. (False) p. 658

27.-.36: What does the word <u>modern</u> mean? Or, to phrase it more precisely, how is the word <u>modern</u> used by historians?

27.-.37: Compare and contrast the developments in the sciences during the twentieth century with the developments in the arts, both popular and elite. Are we living in an age of reason, or of unreason?

27.-.38: Describe and critique the philosophies of history which are grouped under the rubric of "historicism."

27.-.39: Compare and contrast the vision of a single "Western" civilization with that of a world culture. Has the twentieth century brought these competing concepts toward a convergence?

27.-.40: Though the revolution in physics in the twentieth century is very complex, it has had some important practical applications. Identify three of these and discuss their historical importance.

27.-.41: Looking at the general question of the "quality of life" in Western civilization, write an essay comparing periods from the following list with life in the post-1945 world: Ancient Rome, France during the Middle Ages, Italy during the Renaissance, Germany during the Reformation.

27.-.42: The "social sciences" attempt to apply scientific thought to questions of human behavior. Do you see history as a "social science" or as one of the literary arts? Give specific examples to support your argument.

27.-.43: One can argue that Mickey Mouse is a splendid example of the popular culture of the last half of the twentieth century. Indeed his "magic kingdom" is literally the empire on which the sun never sets. If this is true, what does that tell us about contemporary values?

27.-.44: Write an essay defining the "elite" and the "popular" cultures of the last half of the twentieth century, giving specific historical examples.

27.-.45: Consider that you are looking at the civilization of the 1990s from the year 2090. What do you expect will be the most lasting cultural achievements from our era?

TEST ITEM FILE

CHAPTER 28: OUR TIMES: ARRIVING AT THE PRESENT

28.-.1: An important factor in Great Britain's long delay in entering the European Common Market was the opposition of

(a) the Warsaw Pact
(b) France
(c) West Germany
(d) the United States

(b) p. 662

28.-.2: Voted out of office in 1945, Winston Churchill was replaced as prime minister of England by

(a) Harold Wilson.
(b) Anthony Eden.
(c) Clement Attlee.
(d) Margaret Thatcher.

(c) p. 662

28.-.3: Which of the following was NOT an achievement of the British Labour Party in the years immediately after World War II?

(a) nationalization of the coal and railroad industries
(b) halting the migration of England's best scientists and engineers
(c) the introduction of socialized medicine
(d) expansion and partial democratization of the educational system

(b) p. 662

28.-.4: In 1969, bloodshed in this region was sparked by the anniversary celebration of a military victory won by the soldiers of the English monarch William III.

(a) Scotland
(b) the Netherlands
(c) Wales
(d) Ulster

(d) p. 664

28.-.5: In 1961, in a conflict over apartheid, this state unilaterally withdrew from the British Commonwealth.

(a) India
(b) South Africa
(c) Malaya
(d) New Zealand

(b) p. 664

28.-.6: In 1958 France was saved from a military takeover by

(a) the intervention of the United Nations.
(b) the election of Francois Mitterrand.
(c) the resolute response of Valery Giscard.
d'Estaing
(d) the return from retirement of Charles de Gaulle.

(d) p. 665

28.-.7: The German chancellor whose leadership immediately following World War II contributed greatly to his nation's political and economic revival was

(a) Helmut Schmidt.
(b) Konrad Adenauer.
(c) Willy Brandt.
(d) none of the above.

(b) pp. 666-667

28.-.8: Which of the following was NOT a characteristic of the Italian political scene in the decades since World War II?

(a) frequent terrorism and criminal violence
(b) extensive student unrest
(c) a number of coup attempts by the Communist
Party
(d) a bureaucracy plagued by scandal and
corruption

(c) pp. 668-669

28.-.9: The massive emigration into this land following its granting of independence to Indonesia and Surinam gave rise to racial prejudice.

(a) France
(b) Portugal
(c) Spain
(d) the Netherlands

(d) p. 669

28.-.10: In 1974 the colonial conflict in Angola and Mozambique led to a military coup in

(a) France.
(b) Portugal.

(c) Spain.
(d) England.

(b) p. 671

28.-.11: In 1974 Greece and Turkey clashed over this region

(a) Macedonia
(b) Corfu
(c) Crete
(d) Cyprus

(d) p. 671

28.-.12: Which of the following nations has NOT had a woman as head of state in the years since World War II?

(a) Israel
(b) Great Britain
(c) India
(d) United States

(d) p. 670

28.-.13: Senator Joseph McCarthy's "witch hunts" of the early 1950s were directed against

(a) the military-industrial complex.
(b) the Civil Rights movement and its leaders.
(c) the "welfare state."
(d) those he held to be communists and communist supporters.

(d) p. 672

28.-.14: Formal diplomatic relations between the United States and the Peoples' Republic of China were established during the presidency of

(a) Lyndon Johnson.
(b) John F. Kennedy.
(c) Richard Nixon.
(d) Gerald Ford.

(c) p. 674

28.-.15: President Nixon's status as a politician was severely undermined as a consequence of

(a) his secret involvement in the SALT negotiations.
(b) the Iranian hostage issue.
(c) the Watergate scandal.
(d) his response to the Civil Rights movement.

(c) p. 674

28.-.16: The Shahanshah (King of Kings), Mohammed Reza Pahlavi, fled in 1979 from this kingdom, leaving it in the hands of Shi'ite leaders.

(a) Ethiopia
(b) Turkey
(c) Lebanon
(d) Iran

(d) p. 676

28.-.17: Which of the following was a problem confronting Canada in the years after World War II?

(a) slow economic growth
(b) inability to develop its mineral resources
(c) a foreign policy closely tied to that of Great Britain
(d) a separatist movement in the province of Quebec

(d) p. 677

28.-.18: "Ask not what your country can do for you; ask what you can do for your country." These are the words of

(a) Winston Churchill
(b) Charles de Gaulle
(c) John F. Kennedy
(d) Mikhail Gorbachev

(c) p. 675

28.-.19: The "de-Stalinization" program in the Soviet Union was given strong impetus by

(a) Khrushchev.
(b) Kosygin.
(c) Malenkov.
(d) Beria.

(a) p. 678

28.-.20: "Sputnik" signaled the entry of the Soviet Union into the

(a) atomic age.
(b) space age.
(c) Warsaw Pact.
(d) none of the above.

(b) p. 679

28.-.21: Which of the following Soviet citizen's activities were NOT reflective of intellectual unrest in the post-World War II Soviet Union?

(a) Andrei Sakharov

(b) Evgeny Yevtushenko
(c) Alexander Solzhenitsyn
(d) Yuri Andropov

(d) pp. 679-680

28.-.22: The new openness in the Soviet Union, marked by the policies of perestroika and glasnost, was the creation of

(a) Yegor Ligachev.
(b) Eduard Shevardnadze.
(c) Mikhail Gorbachev.
(d) Boris Yeltsin.

(c) p. 680

28.-.23: During the late 1980s, the disintegration of communism in eastern Europe could be seen in which of the following countries?

(a) Hungary
(b) Czechoslovakia
(c) Romania
(d) all of the above

(d) p. 681

28.-.24: Following World War II Tokyo grew to be the largest city in the world until, in 1980, it was surpassed by

(a) Rio de Janeiro.
(b) Mexico City.
(c) Calcutta.
(d) London.

(b) p. 684

28.-.25: The greatest strain on United States-Japanese relations by 1990 came as a result of which of the following?

(a) recurrent political scandals
(b) disputes over fishing rights
(c) environmental concerns
(d) all of the above

(d) p. 685

28.-.26: In 1965, 300,000 communists perished when their planned coup failed in this land.

(a) Malaysia
(b) Ceylon
(c) the Philippines
(d) Indonesia

(d) p. 687

28.-.27: With the flight of Ferdinand Marcos in 1986, Corazon Aquino was recognized by many as the president of this nation.

(a) Taiwan
(b) the Philippines
(c) Singapore
(d) Pakistan

(b) p. 687

28.-.28: The question of Kashmir remains a point of conflict between these two nations.

(a) Malaysia and Indonesia
(b) India and Pakistan
(c) India and Ceylon
(d) Iran and Iraq

(b) p. 688

28.-.29: Pakistan lost considerable, if poverty and conflict-ridden, territory when this region became an independent state.

(a) Afghanistan
(b) Bangladesh
(c) Burma
(d) Ceylon

(b) p. 688

28.-.30: In 1984 Prime Minister Indira Ghandi of India was assassinated by extremists of this group.

(a) Bengals
(b) Afghans
(c) Sikhs
(d) Muslims

(c) p. 688

28.-.31: In 1952 the corrupt monarchy of Egypt was overthrown in a military coup led by

(a) Gamal Abdel Nasser.
(b) Anwar Sadat.
(c) U Thant.
(d) Habib Bourguiba.

(a) p. 690

28.-.32: In 1978, responding to an invitation by President Jimmy Carter, they met at Camp David to establish more harmonious relations between their two countries.

(a) King Hussein and Nasser
(b) Menachim Begin and Anwar Sadat
(c) Yasir Arafat and Idi Amin
(d) Qaddafi and Boumedienne

(b) p. 691

28.-.33: In 1963 Martin Luther King referred to "a promise that all men, yes, black men as well as white men, would be guaranteed the inalienable rights of life, liberty, and the pursuit of happiness." He was referring to

(a) ideals of the Lutheran Reformation.
(b) ideals of the Enlightenment.
(c) the United Nations Charter.
(d) the Fourteen Points.

(b) p. 673

28.-.34: Which of the following was NOT a result of the 1991 Persian Gulf war against Iraq and Saddam Hussien?

(a) unprecedented pollution from burning oil wells of Kuwait
(b) the influx of millions of Kurdish refugees into Iran and Turkey
(c) the removal of Saddam Hussien as the political leader of Iraq
(d) the validation of the superiority of Western arms and technical expertise

(c) pp. 692-693

28.-.35: English settlers fought against the Mau Maus for many years in this former British colony.

(a) Nigeria
(b) the Union of South Africa
(c) Kenya
(d) the Gold Coast

(c) p. 695

28.-.36: The racial policy known as "apartheid" was a source of turmoil and violence here.

(a) India
(b) Angola
(c) the Union of South Africa
(d) Uganda

(c) p. 696

28.-.37: Which of the following men was NOT associated with the social and political struggles of South Africa?

(a) General Joseph Mobutu

(b) Nelson Mandela
(c) Bishop Desmond Tutu
(d) F.W. de Klerk

(a) p. 697

28.-.38: This Marxist president of Chile was overthrown and slain in a coup in which the United States CIA was involved.

(a) Ernesto Che Guevara
(b) Joaquin Balaguer
(c) Salvador Allende Gossens
(d) Juan Bosch

(c) p. 698

28.-.39: A dictator on the model of Mussolini, he long held the support of the "descamisados" (shirtless ones) in governing Argentina.

(a) Regis Debray
(b) Juan Peron
(c) Roberto Ortiz
(d) Emiliano Zapata

(b) p. 698

28.-.40: In 1982 the Argentine military regime suffered a humiliating defeat at the hands of Great Britain over the issue of

(a) Argentina's efforts to boycott English
imports.
(b) possession of the Falkland Islands.
(c) Argentina's sale of military hardware to the Union of South Africa.
(d) none of the above.

(b) p. 698

28.-.41: In the 1980s, United States military forces invaded both Grenada and

(a) El Salvador.
(b) Haiti.
(c) Jamaica.
(d) Panama.

(d) p. 699

28.-.42: Pope John Paul II is the first non-Italian to hold that office in more than 400 years. (True) p. 669

28.-.43: Germany was reunited swiftly and peacefully after the fall of the Berlin Wall in 1989. (True) p. 668

28.-.44: The 1989 incident in Tiananmen Square severely damaged Chinese-Western relations. (True) p. 685

28.-.45: Nelson Mandela became president of South Africa in 1994 after leading the black majority in a bloody purge of South African whites. (False) p. 697

28.-.46: Marx, Engels, and Lenin all argued that capitalism would fall as the workers of the world rose up and cast off their chains. Where and by what means did Marxism grow between 1945 and 1970? Where and by what means did it lose power in the 1980s and l990s?

28.-.47: Considering the period 1945-1970, compare and contrast the states of the Western bloc and the Eastern bloc in Europe, with regard to their political systems, economic progress, and international arrangements. What factors after 1970 made the states more similar, until by 1990 the "blocs" no longer had their former meaning?

28.-.48: What was the relationship between the Cold War and the end of the old colonial empires?

28.-.49: Consider the "prospects" added at the end of this chapter. What genuine progress has occurred in our history, and why do the authors appear optimistic about the long-term significance of Western civilization and its contributions to the world? Do you agree?

28.-.50: Consider the political problems and opportunities of the current world order (or disorder). Some would argue that every problem has within it an opportunity. Write an essay giving an example of a historic problem/opportunity in the contemporary world.